Gold Scars

GOLD SCARS

THE TRUTH ABOUT
GRIEF, LOSS AND TRAUMA
AND HOW TO BEAUTIFULLY MEND

Sylvia Moore
MYERS

NEW YORK

LONDON • NASHVILLE • MELBOURNE • VANCOUVER

GOLD SCARS

The Truth About Grief. Loss and Trauma and How to Beautifully Mend

Published in New York, New York, by Morgan James Publishing. Morgan James is a trademark of Morgan James, LLC. www.MorganJamesPublishing.com

Scripture taken from the New King James Version® (NKJV). Copyright © 1982 by Thomas Nelson, Inc. Used by permission. All rights reserved.

Scripture quotations marked (NLT) are taken from the Holy Bible, New Living Translation, copyright © 1996, 2004, 2007 by Tyndale House Foundation. Used by permission of Tyndale House Publishers, Inc., Carol Stream, IL 60188. All rights reserved.

Scripture taken from the Holy Bible, Today's New International Version® (NIV). Copyright © 2001, 2005 by Biblica®. Used by permission of Biblica®. All rights reserved worldwide.

Proudly distributed by Publishers Group West®

Morgan James BOGO™

A **FREE** ebook edition is available for you or a friend with the purchase of this print book.

CLEARLY SIGN YOUR NAME ABOVE

Instructions to claim your free ebook edition:
1. Visit MorganJamesBOGO.com
2. Sign your name CLEARLY in the space above
3. Complete the form and submit a photo of this entire page
4. You or your friend can download the ebook to your preferred device

ISBN 9781636982823 paperback
ISBN 9781636982830 ebook
Library of Congress Control Number: 2023946919

Cover and Interior Design by:
Chris Treccani
www.3dogcreative.net

Morgan James is a proud partner of Habitat for Humanity Peninsula and Greater Williamsburg. Partners in building since 2006.

Get involved today! Visit: www.morgan-james-publishing.com/giving-back

TABLE OF CONTENTS

DEDICATION

To God be the Glory. To Christ my Redeemer.

To my best friend and partner in life, Adam Myers. God put you in my life when I was the most broken. You demanded I be strong. There would be no book without you.

To my grown sons, Isaac and Daniel. Thank you for letting me do a fair job of parenting while the three of us grieved. You taught me by your example how to mend.

To my beautiful daughter-in-law Jessica, my grandbabies Ellowyn Noel and Elon Jacob. I am truly blessed to have you in my life. God knew you would shine a light in my path one day.

ACKNOWLEDGMENTS

A special thanks to all the beautiful humans who helped make this book a reality:

--my patient and understanding husband, Adam Myers – you were the fire, the energy and the strength that encouraged me to share my story so others could be healed. Thank you for being my coach, counselor, partner and Jiminy Cricket. Thanks for the "Scruples".

--the talented artist (and my son) Daniel Moore who helped stage my photos and the book cover, who created ALL the Kintsugi art in and on the book, vases, bowls and even my face.

--to Bobby McCullough of Dynes Media, who saw my vision and brought my story to life on the book cover and in film.

--to Jennifer Bace of Nest & Nook who agreed to treat me like a stage prop for the cover.

--to Kelli Glaser for your amazing patience in hair and makeup (I promise not to cut my own bangs again).

xii | G<small>OLD</small> S<small>CARS</small>

--to my friends and family Adam, Jessica, Isaac, Daniel, Dawn Melden, Laura and Lauren McCullough, who practice "Presentness" – for you, I am truly blessed.

--to my many family members, friends, lost loves, and everyone mentioned (and not mentioned) in this book – you touched my life, so I thank you.

--To all my friends at Best Seller Publishing – thank you for standing by me (pushing me) as I wrote this book.

--To all my friends at Morgan James Publishing – thank you for your confidence in me and this message and for taking me over the finish line.

--to anyone I have not mentioned. Please write your name in this blank: _____ This book is for you.

INTRODUCTION

Why You Should
Read This Book

How many books have been written on HOW TO HEAL from grief, loss, and trauma? There's always a new and improved way of Healing or Overcoming the Odds. The Wounded, the Broken-Hearted? We have read them all. Searching for that Secret. And while I have learned so much about my grief, loss, and the traumas, I have still suffered.

What if I told you that we never *really* heal from grief, loss, or trauma? Not *really*. There will always be scars as we never forget what happened to us, or to the ones we loved.

Now, what if I also told you, "It's Okay to Scar"?

We can embrace Scars! Fill those bad boys with Gold, like a Japanese Kintsugi vase or bowl, and just wear them like Gold Battle Scars. Got your attention?

I'd like to suggest to you that the reason you cannot *heal* is because you cannot *heal*. That healing is not possible with time nor methods. In fact, it takes courage to acknowledge our grief, loss, and trauma and live in our grief, and only then can we find healing and look at our wounds differently. I believe we were created to scar, not heal. We were ALWAYS meant to SCAR. So SCAR!!!!

Why GOLD SCARS?

As I mentioned, Kintsugi is a Japanese tradition that says we do not discard that which is broken; instead, we mend with gold a cherished bowl or vase when it breaks, leaving Gold Scars. Beautifully mended, our Gold Scarred container is ready to be cherished and filled once again.

We are also made from clay, just like bowls and vases. God placed our spirit inside these cherished containers that can never *really* heal. On Purpose.

Lucky is the chameleon who grows back the part he loses. Remarkable is the sea cucumber who can mend its organs and heal from near fatal wounds in about a week's time. But we, God's beloved, were meant to scar. A testimony of our life and the trials and tribulations that we experience. A reminder that only God can truly heal us. He reminds us in scripture that our souls are eternal, not our containers. Wasn't it Christ Himself who showed His scars from the cross to Timothy? After His resurrection, His wounds were healed, His life restored, but the GOLD SCARS remained.

We are not the only creatures on Earth that scar. So, be thankful God did not give us a new ring around our backs every year of life like the turtle. We'd never be able to lie about our age.

Scars on the heart are harder to share, but they are there. There is no sense trying to hide them. Recovery and healing come from the courage of owning and naming the scar.

I'm scarred but healed. I'm wounded but mended. See my Gold Scars? Have courage and show me yours. And let me show you how to be a Gold Scar Survivor.

THE TRUTH

When we grieve, when we experience incredible, life-shaking trauma, we have very little resources or people to which to turn. There are few if any who understand what we are going through. What's said by family and friends is almost always "the wrong thing to say."

Although your close friends and family want to help, your pain is misunderstood by the masses. But you need help. You need something. Not cards or a rehashed cliché. Not sympathy or false promises. If you have suffered a tragic loss, right now, your world is burning around you, and no one showed up to the funeral or the hospital with water. Just words.

Many counselors will tell you there are stages of grief and trauma. If they believe they are truly *learned*, they will give you the name of the psychiatrist who designed those stages (Elisabeth Kübler-Ross, 1969, *On Death and Dying*). But what they forget is that she never meant for her stages of grief, originally focused on the terminally ill, to be applied to the masses.

For years, this sent grieving children, parents, and lovers down the spiral path to despair, thinking there is something terribly wrong with them for not "healing" in the right order or the correct time frame. The pain and the scars mounted up, and there was no clear path to healing.

What Kübler-Ross did get right were the emotions behind trauma and loss. We all *feel* denial, anger, bargaining, depression, and acceptance at one point or another during our time in grief or trauma. But the order, magnitude, and time spent with each emotion is different for everyone.

Like delicate bowls that fall onto hard surfaces, we break differently, uniquely. We start picking up the broken pieces trying unsuccessfully to erase the damage. But we cannot. Like the cherished broken bowl that we cannot throw away, let me show you how to fill the scars with Gold as you heal.

HOW YOU WILL RECOVER

How can you heal? Can you get better? Do you "recover"? Can you, as some professionals instruct, walk away from grief and trauma? Here's a surprise: there is a path to healing, but walking away is not going to get you there.

There is no instant fix to what hurts you, no quick solution to the loss of someone you love. No one will find that place missing or broken in your heart and heal it right up. We do not forget or move on or around the loss and grief from horrible events. No matter what you have heard from friends, pastors, or inspirational speakers, your ship is not coming in. There is no pot of gold at the end of the rainbow or silver lining on your rain cloud. There's no fairy godmother standing by to erase the wrong. And, as skilled as they may be, there are some things doctors, pastors, friends, and even fairy godmothers cannot fix.

However, you can, with a little help, find the right path to heal, be healthy, stay hopeful, experience God's holiness, live happily, and even be hilarious again.

So put on the red shoes, Dorothy, and let me show you a way to look at the grief in a new light, which can lead you on the path to recovery. You can face anything that belongs to you. And grief, loss, heartache, and trauma do indeed belong to you.

Who am I? My name is Sylvia Moore Myers. I'm an author, speaker, and coach with The Maxwell Leadership team as well as a certified Advanced Grief Recovery Specialist, and the Founder of Gold Scars and 7 to Heal. And I have been at the hospital holding my teenage son's hand, knowing this was the last time I would see him alive. I shopped for a coffin before his body was cold. I've said goodbye to my dearest friend, buried both my parents, two brothers, and a sister—all too young to die. I've suffered the trauma and pain of losing an unborn child. Faced sincere heartbreak. Lived through sexual harassment and bullying. I've faced and overcome cancer. Eight months after the death of my child, I survived a physical attack on my life, with my children only feet away as I fought to escape.

I've been on all sides of grief and trauma. And I want you to hear about loss and recovery from someone who really *does* understand.

This book is a result of a lifetime of learning about grief and loss and discovering the path to true healing. I will share my experiences and what happened on my journey where I healed. I'll also share how I discovered what I call the 7 to Heal: Help, Healing, Healthy, Hope, Holiness, and Happiness—I'll even show you how to be Hilarious again. But moreover, I want to help you take your trauma and grief with you on this true journey to recovery where a little courage, some action, and acceptance can turn your wounds into Gold Scars.

I have made it my life's goal to help you learn to recover and be whole again. I'm not talking about forgetting or ridding yourself of the past but learning to properly carry your trials, tribulations, and even triumphs with you on life's journey—and how to keep the traumatic events, which are a normal part of life, from preventing you from living a healthy, happy, and very successful life.

By learning to give, forgive, and live again, you can find healing and happiness you might have thought you would never experience again.

Disclaimer 1: If you are one of the lucky people who have yet to experience great loss or grief, you will. You most assuredly will. From my research, there are over 40 different causes of grief. Grief and trauma recovery are normal parts of life. How our society, worldwide, deals with grief and trauma can make recovery difficult, if not impossible.

Disclaimer 2: If you believe you are required to be forever sad, you are simply a little lost. Let me get you back on that path. Plus, learning how to first help yourself with pain, grief, loss, and trauma will not only heal you but will also prepare you to be that loving, caring, empathetic friend for others one day.

Pick up your pain, loss, trauma, grief, and the broken pieces of your heart and take them on this journey with me. Give yourself permission to dream. Learn to forgive. Be compassionate toward yourself and others. Stop bargaining with God about the past and learn to be excited about the future. Smile again. Remember, there is always room for laughter. Does this sound unbelievable? You're only in the prologue.

The right road to surviving and thriving is just ahead. No stopwatches, no tests, and no limitations. Just you and me looking at the 7 to Heal: Help, Healing, Healthy, Hope, Holiness, and Happiness, learning to be Hilarious again, and mending our life, hearts, and wounds with Gold Scars.

PART 1:

I'd Like to Order a Slice of Self-Loathing

T ruth be told, my personal trauma and subsequent unresolved grief began very early in my life. My story is like
that of many others. Years of pain and loss with no one
to blame but myself. The traumas I witnessed, the pain I suffered,
and the losses I endured piled up over the years, peaking with a
tragic death of a child followed by a physical attack on me in my
own driveway. Here is my story and how I tried to heal.

My family volunteered as first responders throughout my late
childhood, and I personally volunteered as an EMT cadet on
the City Volunteer Life Squad from age 15 to adulthood. I saw a
plethora of tragedies and traumas, blunt trauma injuries, broken
bones, heart attacks, and burns. Coming home washing someone
else's blood off your jumpsuit or discussing CPR and tourniquets
at the dinner table were normal events for my family. At 15, I
thought I knew about grief and trauma.

In the late 1970s, my parents and older brother, Bob, fought
the Beverly Hills Country Club fire in Northern Kentucky beside
hundreds of other firefighters and first responders across the
tri-state area. I watched the live coverage on television with my
younger siblings from home. Bob told me many years later that he
had recurring dreams of the charred bodies he had pulled from the
building after the fire had been subdued. First responders often
experience night terrors, grief, and PTSD after a tragedy. My parents, brother, and I were no exception.

At age 12, I helped care for my infant brother, Jeff, who suffered from a severe form of sleep apnea and stopped breathing
almost nightly. The monitors attached to him with wires and
sticky patches would scream out the evening event, waking the
entire family and a few of the neighbors. We had a special bat-
tery-operated monitor that set off an alarm should the electricity
go out. Between the fire-department monitors, breathing moni-

tors, and power-outage monitors, it was a miracle anyone slept in that house. My family decided we would take shifts to listen, as a preemptive strategy to hush the nightly alarms.

My watch was after dinner until 11 p.m. on school days and 9 p.m. to 2 a.m. on weekends. I would sit beside Jeff's crib and study or watch TV but with the sound down so I could hear every breath he took. If he failed to breathe, I would lift him from the bed, maybe give him mouth-to-mouth once or twice, and he would start breathing again. Sometimes, I would just reach through the bars of his crib and pat him on the butt or shake his leg, and he would take a healthy breath of air into his lungs. Jeff *was* a full-time job for several years. Years later, as each of my children was born, I spent many sleepless nights hovering over their cribs—my ear close to their faces, making sure they were breathing.

Death first hit close to home when my grandmother died. I was eight years old. We shared the same first name, last name, and appearance, and I loved her. She had been my comforter and my hero, and when she left I felt lonely. I dreamed of her often after she died. Dreams took me back to her little country kitchen in Hamilton, Ohio, where I sat on the red step stool chair eating cookies.

Two years ago, when we purchased our little farm, I bought a red Stylaire retro two-step chair for my kitchen. My grandbabies sit on it and eat cookies. So do I.

Sometime in my tweens, Tracy, an older teen and friend from church, took her own life. I was told she was broken-hearted over a lost boyfriend. I attended Tracy's funeral at our church and worried that this might be normal for older girls. She had given me her coveted Trixie Belden books, some really groovy '60s clothes, and a few dolls that I loved. Her disturbing death would trouble me for years. There were no discussions or normalizing of these types of events in my home. Death, dying, and any strong emotion was simply accepted and then properly dismissed. Washed down the drain like blood from an ambulance trip.

Later, as a practicing trial paralegal, I helped women and men escape abusive relationships and seek comfort. I assisted in wrongful death claims and personal injury, criminal defense, and domestic abuse cases. One of the attorneys for whom I worked was shot in his law office by an angry future ex-husband of his divorce client. A depressed client hanged himself in the county jail using the clothes we had just taken him to wear to trial.

I viewed photos from cases too gruesome and disgusting to describe. A child killed by a falling tree cut down by his father and uncle. An infant strangled in his car seat while his mother was in the other room gathering laundry. Pornography from the infamous Newport Northern Kentucky dirty bookstore case that could only be described as "yuck" by an innocent 18-year-old working part-time in the law-office file room after school. Yup, me. Forty-two years later, I can still picture that horrible "yuck."

By my 20s, I had endured a cheating husband, a broken heart, an unwanted abortion, bullying, work and teacher sexual harassment, a cancer diagnosis, and several toxic relationships. I unknowingly suffered from Stockholm syndrome and PTSD.

I was not prepared for personal loss and trauma. Instead of seeking help to recover and understand my losses as they occurred, I just stood in my own way to recovery and happiness. I barred the door to healing by accepting my pain and suffering as recompense for some sin I'd committed in life. I resolved that I had lost any chance to enjoy God's holiness because of my past transgressions. I dropped out of college, forfeited my dream career, and allowed myself to splash about in my bowl of self-loathing.

My soul was broken. Although I acted the part of a saved and happy Christian woman, I was empty from my past losses and pain. So I sought the things of the world to fill the cracks in my heart and soul.

Even as a Christian, I was low on Jesus, and I needed to be filled by God. But I felt unworthy. I'm sure if I had a guardian angel back then, he was standing in the back of the room of Heaven shrugging his shoulders whenever God asked, "How's Sylvia?"

While my life had been one heartbreak after another, I somehow felt I had made it through to the other side each time. I thought I was resilient and strong. I thought I had seen the worst. I thought wrong. I had serious, deep scars. I was bruised on the inside and the outside. I was doing what my family taught me to do with grief and loss: accept it, wash it down the drain, and promptly dismiss it. "Move on."

And "Move on" I did. In May 2003, with three beautiful sons, a kind husband, and a thriving real-estate brokerage, I was at the top of my game. I was running 10K a week, eating healthily, and living a good life. At first blush, I appeared to have my life together. *Tout au contraire*; I was broken inside at this point in my life. I just did not see it.

Having never resolved the heartaches and pain from my past, I carried each new and exciting traumatic event in my arms and dumped the whole mess into each new relationship or endeavor. But in 2003 and the months that followed, I would suffer terrible grief and trauma that would change the course of my life forever. I would discover how broken I really was and how much more broken I could become. My fragile bowl was falling to that hard surface below. But here's the thing: by really hitting bottom, by truly living inside my grief, I would also learn how to truly recover. And how to help others.

FIRSTBORN SONS

In May 2003, my mother's firstborn son and my eldest brother, Marvin, (we called him "Bo") passed away under my watch due to complications from mold poisoning and years of smoking. Bo had taken a job as a plane mechanic in a Valdosta, Georgia, airline hangar, 700 miles from my parents' home in Kentucky and over 1,200 miles from his five grown children in Boston. He listed me as the nearest living relative when he was admitted to the hospital. They researched and finally found me. I got the call, and after the "What the heck? How did he get to Georgia?" moment passed, I set out for Valdosta to find Bo.

I had moved to Georgia from Northern Kentucky in the early '90s when my husband took a teaching job in Middle Georgia. So, I was taken aback that Bo had recently moved to South Georgia without telling me or the rest of the family.

I traveled nearly every day to visit him, two hours in each direction. He was always in a good mood, laughing with the nurses and playing the guitar that my firstborn son, Jacob, had given him. The mess pumped from his lungs resembled incredibly old chocolate milk. His prognosis was not good, but there was hope.

He had been away from his little rental home for quite some time, and we were concerned about his belongings. We found his house near Valdosta, but it had been completely cleaned out while he was in the hospital. Years of aircraft mechanic tools, clothes, memories, and his personal guitar—gone. The only possessions he had at that moment were his wallet and the clothes he'd worn when admitted to the ICU.

But Bo seemed joyful despite the loss. One day, Bo brought up God. He wanted to know about Jesus and wondered why he had never been baptized. We called the hospital chaplain, and Bo insisted on being baptized right in that hospital bed.

A few days afterward, Bo's condition deteriorated, and he went into a coma. His foot had turned gangrenous, so I signed the document that allowed the surgeon to remove his leg at the knee.

Miraculously, Bo awoke from the coma a few days later, and the first words he whispered to me were "Where is my leg, sis?" He chuckled and gave me a reassuring smile.

"We have the staff looking for it, Bo—I'm sure it will turn up," I teased as I acted out looking under his bed and inside a few drawers for the forlorn leg.

"Well, I hope not," he announced. "I was hoping for a nice bionic leg like the six-million-dollar man. I have plans, you know, to run in the next Boston Marathon." We both laughed at the thought.

"Let's get you home first, Bo."

We immediately made plans to fly him to the VA hospital in Lexington, Kentucky, to be near our parents. Bo was a Marine Vietnam vet. A local retired Air Force pilot offered to fly us there and bring me back on his personal plane. Bo was excited. Our parents were elated. Both our parents had serious health issues at the time that made a trip to Southern Georgia impossible.

The hospital readied what we would need for the ambulance ride to the airport and the flight to Kentucky. I packed Bo's new Bible, his newly acquired guitar, and some new clothes for the trip. The morning of the flight, I said goodbye to my family, and was on my long drive to the Valdosta airport when the hospital called.

Marvin "Bo" Keith Bowman had passed away suddenly. A blood clot from what was left of his leg had traveled to his heart, taking his life instantly. I was so angry. Angry at myself, the doctors, Bo ... and I didn't know why. I continued my drive, but to arrange for Bo's body to be transported to Kentucky for a funeral.

I barely made it through the call to my dad and mom, explaining that Bo was not flying home in a private jet to reunite with them, that instead he was on a train in a coffin. They had lost their firstborn son. My mother was devastated — heartbroken. If only we had known what was coming around the bend, I could have warned her to "Hunker down, Betty, there's more grief on the horizon."

LOVE, LOSS, AND HEARTBREAK

Big John was tall, dark, and handsome. The Prince Charming most little girls dream about. The gallant young prince who sweeps you off your feet from his stallion and makes you queen of all you survey. I met Prince Charming in the school band room in June 1980. Both of us had graduated from high school weeks earlier. We were just visiting old friends, saying goodbye, and preparing for college in the fall.

John Works had moved to Florida two years previously when his dad took a new job, but after his father died unexpectedly, John, his mom, and little brother moved back to Northern Kentucky to be closer to extended family. I remembered him as an awkward 16-year-old when he left, but now he was a distinguished older teen with a full beard and a smile that could melt icebergs.

High school was a whirlwind for me. I decided to join everything the last two years of school. I left after my senior year with a long list of accomplishments: student council president, field commander of the band, Miss Scott High School, and homecoming court. I wrote the school fight song and helped orchestrate the first parade down the middle of a major highway in the city of Taylor Mill, all while staying on the honor roll.

Betty, my mom and mother of ten, was running for mayor of Taylor Mill. She had been a city council member and had served as police commissioner and as a volunteer for the life squad and fire department; later, she would assist the governor of Kentucky and consider a senate run. My dad, Bob, was a supervisor at a large corporation, served as fire chief, volunteered for the local life squad, and sat on the Dan Beard Boy Scout council. In later years, Dad wrote for newspapers and authored many short stories. Thus, I was from a family of smart overachievers. College was waiting and paid for—by me.

I had landed a legal secretary position with a downtown law firm months before high school graduation—a steppingstone to my future career as an attorney and my loftier goal of Supreme Court justice. "I am going to *hear* the big cases, not *try* them," I used to brag.

That summer, I really did not have a care in the world. And I did not expect the events that would change all of my plans and dreams and send me in the wrong direction.

It was love at first sight—for me, at least. Within a month, John and I were together almost every day. We had a fun summer, talked about where we might live, hung out, made out, and tried to figure out the future. He signed up for classes. I purchased books and started my first semester at Northern Kentucky University. Everything was *keikaku doori* (falling into place as planned).

It was the missed period that caught me off-guard. My periods had been on point since noon on my 13th birthday. I seriously did not expect to get pregnant. I couldn't get pregnant, right? I was living the *Legally Blonde* movie and the "Perfect Day" song in my mind, so the thought of being pregnant had not factored into my plan for acquiring a Supreme Court seat. I broke the news to John immediately.

Big John thought this through, and within a few days gave me his decision. He found a clinic over the river in Cincinnati that would be happy to end the pregnancy. "No big deal," they said, "it's so early, there's just nothing there but a little tissue." John seemed convinced.

I had never given abortion much thought. I was raised a strict Protestant in a mostly Catholic neighborhood. In our town, you might go away for a while if you are pregnant, but ending a pregnancy—well, that was not up for discussion. It was simply not an option.

Betty, the high-IQ mother of ten, and Bob, the overachiever father, never discussed abortion. There were no mother-daughter, father-daughter here-is-what-you-do-to-prevent-pregnancy or this-is-what-you-do-if-you-get-pregnant discussions. Neither was it okay to come talk to Betty or Bob if anything like pregnancy happened. Nothing was discussed, and I was clueless as to what to do next.

Betty was not a girlie girl by any means. Although she dressed the part of *une professionnelle féminine* every day, she practically wrote the book on how to be a successful businesswoman in a '70s and '80s man's world while raising those ten children. Voted into office as Major by Write-in Vote, Betty was intellectually gifted. Somewhere during this time, my mother received a coveted Mother of the Year award from our Greater Cincinnati–Northern Kentucky newspaper.

Betty had traveled with the first woman governor of Kentucky, had meetings all over the tri-state area with various mayors, state representatives, congresspersons, and the media, and she had attended important political events in many cities, including

Washington, DC. Betty and I had business discussions, political discussions, and etiquette and travel discussions, but sex, marriage, and pregnancy were off the table—especially in the wrong socially acceptable order. I could properly set a table for a multi-course meal, but I had no idea how to talk to my mother.

I envied other girls for their relationships with their mothers. Shopping, chatting, doing mother-daughter things were unknown to me. When this all hit the fan, I made a business decision to table this *pregnancy* matter for a future discussion, manage it on my own, or talk to Dad.

When my first period arrived at lunchtime on my 13th birthday, it was Dad who was there to pick me up from junior high school and drive me to the drugstore to buy feminine hygiene products. Dad was typically the one who took me shopping and purchased dresses for every teen dance, prom, and important social event. My older sisters had paved the way for me to learn that Dad was the one to bring to such a shopping event—not Mom.

Dad also helped me get an honorary Eagle Scout award from his Boy Scout troop. He taught me how to speak French and Japanese, hit a baseball like a college pro, and how to defend myself. He laughingly encouraged me to marry a Boy Scout if I got a chance and even suggested he should pick the fellow out for me. Dad trusted me to make sound logical decisions, including not having sex before marriage, but it was not discussed, only assumed like my good grades and being in before 9 p.m. on a school night except during marching-band season.

I decided to keep the pregnancy off the family table and handle this perceived failure on my own. I simply had no intention of damaging Mom's political career or breaking Dad's heart.

In the alternative, I sought out my employer for advice. Besides being my first boss, Bill was a practicing Catholic, a remarkable trial attorney, and a beloved and trusted neighbor. I had always relied on his advice in the past and knew it was truly confidential. "Abortion is legal," he counseled me. "Why let an unexpected pregnancy screw up your future when things are looking so bright?"

Although this seemed well intended advice, inside my brain, everything was wrong. There was a screaming voice, a persistent noise that said, "Stop. Don't do this. It's wrong. You will regret it. This IS a baby! This is MY baby." You can argue anything you like among yourselves about what I was thinking, but this was a normal reaction of me protecting my child. This was also the quiet, still voice of God trying to change my path.

There was no one else who was pointing me in any other direction. But I pushed back and decided against abortion. This was not what I wanted for me, my body, or my baby. I was the proverbial Horton, holding up my dust speck, yelling: "A person's a person, no matter how small!"

But Big John convinced me that the decision was important to him, that at the very least we attend the free counseling session with the clinic. Fear of losing him settled in and there I sat with Big John beside me in front of this 20-something counselor sitting in a chair, her legs crossed, holding a clipboard in her lap, and smiling a pretty smile.

The counselor explained the process would be as pain-free as a tooth filling and even faster for recovery. She said she was working on her medical career, and if she were to discover herself pregnant, she and her fiancé would not think twice about ending the pregnancy before they were ready to have a baby. "There's nothing there but a few cells," she said as she handed me brochures with pictures of happy, childless women.

Not everyone claims to have feelings for the unborn, or the aborted child. But I did. And for that I have no apologies, only grief. This is a normal and natural reaction for many—if not most women and men—to feel failure, loss, depression, or trauma because of an abortion, whether intentional or a miscarriage.

I could not see it then, but the counselor was wrong. There was nothing in her pamphlets about how it might screw up your life and destroy your self-image and lower your self-worth, or how this would kick-start a lifetime of self-loathing and self-destruction.

What would further keep me from healing from this trauma was the divisive opinions of the masses toward abortion. The sides were divided equally in battle. I felt I had no one to talk to about it. I had my dust speck held high on a clover, but I was being pulled back and forth by the forces. "Boil that dust speck," Miss Clipboard said. There was no JoJo to "yopp" to the masses. No heartbeat or swish or any sound out of my baby. If only I'd had Horton's courage at the age of 18.

Society told me abortion was embarrassing, and I should never discuss it again. Or no one can know because it is unimportant. They will laugh at you if you claim you are sad or hurt or injured. Abortion is forgettable—just cells. Get over it. What's done is done. Move on. It is socially unacceptable to say anything against abortion. After all, it was made legal by the very panel of judges with whom you desire membership.

Religion made me feel I could never confess to anyone, or I would be judged a killer and kicked out of church and Heaven in that order. And forget about volunteering for children's church or the nursery. No decent Christian mother would let me within a mile of her unaborted baby.

My self-imposed punishment was to try to stop thinking about it, while telling myself that the way I felt was selfish and self-indulgent. If God would forgive me, all this turmoil would fade from memory. But because I had nightmares about it almost every night, God must hate me, and I would probably go to Hell. The special Hell where baby killers and failures hang out.

Obviously, I surmised, I didn't deserve any more children. Look what I'd done with the first one. Failure. I didn't deserve to go back to college—failure. I was unworthy of all things good because I was—a failure.

If only someone had intervened. If only someone had offered to help me afterward. If only someone … But no one said to me, "How do you feel, Sylvia? Are you okay? It's okay to feel pain over this child's loss." I felt that I was set up to be ostracized by both sides on the sidewalks of abortion clinics everywhere. I was not permitted to feel like what had happened to me was wrong. I was not permitted to feel like I was grieving. But wrong was how I felt, and the grief was overwhelming.

Miss Clipboard was wrong. Pain was involved from the moment that doctor touched the inside of my womb—physical pain and emotional pain. And that pain remained for a very long time. The noise of the machine tearing up my child rang in my ears for years. My guardian angel stepped outside the throne room to cry.

The pain of losing a child is still present, and I think about my child (whom I named Adrianna) often. I did talk with God, and I did find peace and forgiveness. But the journey to peace took a very long, lonely, and dark broken road of self-loathing, sadness, and feelings of unworthiness.

I thought I had completely failed as a mother. And while I would find the truth many years later, the happy, healthy, hopeful, overachieving young lady I had been now felt broken, helpless, and alone in my shame.

I would not tell the world about this event for many, many years. How do you answer someone who asks, "How many children do you have?" Do I count my aborted child? Will that open a conversation I cannot bear? It was easier to keep silent. I hid the truth and began a lifetime of lying to others and myself about what had happened.

SALT IN THE WOUNDS

N ow, back in the early '80s, surrounded by church, family, and the nosy neighbors, you got yourself married when you got pregnant or had a child, even if no one knew about the baby.

Our families were well respected in Northern Kentucky. It seemed the logical, politically correct thing to do. My parents were confused and concerned and insisted I finish college and continue my career. But John and I went through with the marriage anyway.

Big John bought me a dinky ring. I did not care at the time. I was marrying my Prince Charming. I was still in deep depression from the loss of the baby and with zero support or comfort from any direction. I dropped all my classes at NKU and thought myself unworthy to be a student of higher learning at that time.

There was some unknown, undiscussed reason that I felt I must suffer for some unknown, undiscussed time. And I did suffer. At least, I thought, I would have Big John, and my life was not a complete failure.

We were married in February 1981, on Valentine's Day. I had just turned 19 a month before and still had not signed back up for university. Big John was working at the hospital in Covington, Kentucky, and I was still working at the attorney's office downtown typing, filing, reading case law, and dreaming about a career I felt I no longer deserved.

We were married with all the normal pomp and circumstance, and showered with wedding gifts and well wishes from family, friends, and politicians all over the tri-state area. We moved into a cool upstairs flat in the city, got a cat and a pool table, and settled into the married life you might expect from a couple of teenagers.

Not long after the wedding, my brother Bob called me. Bobby and I were born about 18 months apart, and we were very close. He was an early walker, and I was an early talker. We played together, read together, and hung out together. I have no memories of my early childhood when Bobby was not present.

"I need to talk with you right away," Bobby started. "Can you come by my apartment?" Bobby worked at the same hospital as Big John. Bobby was working and going to college at NKU full-time, getting closer to his master's in marketing.

At his apartment, Bobby explained to me that a friend from work had sat with him and others in the hospital cafeteria the previous day, showing off her new engagement ring. Bobby acted out her scene by lifting his ring finger in the air for all to adore. "It was a spectacular ring, hunky-chunky diamond and all," Bobby explained. "Wow," he asked the lady, "who's the lucky guy?" "Big John," she proudly announced. Taken aback, Bob asked, "He works here? At the hospital? That John?" "Yes, that's him," she said—the two lovebirds had been seeing each other for months, blah, blah, blah. "Well, what a coincidence," Bob revealed, "that's my brother-in-law!"

"You should have seen the look on her face!" Bob was almost laughing but stopped short when he got a good look at me.

My face was red—my eyes were welling up with tears, and I was forcing small breaths of air into my closing windpipe. I heard him. But it took a minute of silence before the ground beneath my feet started to shift. My tall, dark, and handsome was using me, lying to me, cheating on me, and eventually divorcing me. I had already suspected something was wrong, not by direct proof, but I'd hoped it was me overthinking and being too needy. I had been accused of both recently by my tall, dark, and handsome.

The world I knew was crashing in. I had lost a baby. I had dropped out of college and recently sold my books. Many of my friends had moved on to college or jobs. I had lost so much, just to lose so much again. But I was losing my Prince Charming, and it was salt in my open wounds. So I drove to my parents' home and sat in my father's arms and cried for hours.

REVENGE IS A DISH BEST
SERVED WITH A COLD BEER

L ater that evening, I dried my tears and headed back to town. Big John was not at home, but I found him, nonetheless, sitting in the local bar, a hunky-chunky beside him, cold beers in a bucket of ice on the table. I punched him square in the jaw, then followed up with a beer-and-ice shower over his head. It was refreshing—for me.

While I do not recommend punching your cheating husband in front of his fiancée, I do believe I saw a falling star on my way back to my car. I dusted the star off, put it in my pocket, and drove home to pack.

At 19, having already lived with a ton of pain, I became a doormat, ready for dirty feet. And there were many feet lining up to step on me in the not-so-distant future.

NOT A GOOD DATE

After my big breakup and heartbreak with Big John, I floated about, waiting for our attorneys to divvy up the expensive, mostly unopened, or unused wedding gifts and the joint bank accounts. Friends and family set me up with blind dates: a politician, a mathematician, and an engineer. Each was interesting and interested in me, but besides my obvious lack of interest in the opposite sex, they were all older than me, and quite honestly, I was still a child. A very injured child at that.

My heart was still broken, and my ability to communicate with the opposite sex was impaired. I was not a good date. Why is it, when someone's heart is crushed, the whole world thinks the best medicine is another relationship? It is like asking a plane crash survivor if they want to jump on the next flight with you. "Come one, scaredy cat, it was just a little crash. You should not take it so seriously. Look at the fun you are missing."

I tortured myself with a few casual dates—going to dinner occasionally with a friend from my local fire department until he confessed that he was engaged. I dated a friend from high school until he told me he was still in love with his high school girlfriend.

21

Fine. Lucky girl. They are still married today. I tried to rekindle a relationship with my high school boyfriend, Sean. But he had already made a commitment to another. They are still married, and we are still friends. Fine.

Our office FedEx delivery guy asked me out, and after several casual lunch dates, I was starting to really like him. We had a dinner date coming up, and I realized I had a conflict. He had always called me from his work phone, so I used all my paralegal investigation skills to discover his house phone number, only to have his wife answer. Yep—no kidding! She sure was surprised. I hope she punched him square in the jaw. He never delivered another package to our office after that day. Weird, huh?

The state of my heart was broken. I was already a small doormat in my mind, so why would anyone in their *right* mind want to get serious with a loser like me? I resolved to stay single and just entertain my baby brothers for the rest of the summer by taking them shopping or to the zoo or whatever I could find to pass the time until I got back to college in the fall.

JOHN 2.0

(Note: When writing a book, don't admit to marrying two guys named John. It drives your editor and publisher crazy. But here we go anyway.)

John 2.0 had been a good friend during high school. We had tried dating briefly back then, but mutually decided we were better just being friends. He had joined the U.S. Army right after graduation and had spent the last two years stationed in Germany.

He was heading to Louisiana in the Fall but was working the rest of the Summer at the Army recruitment center in Northern Kentucky so he could get reacquainted with family and friends. He asked me out.

We had a blast that summer: fishing, cooking out, watching movies. Whatever we wanted to do. And I felt happy again, with someone who was not engaged or in love with anyone else.

What happens to a seriously depressed woman who has lost a child and a man she loves in less than a year? She rebounds. I should have been back in college. I should have sought counseling and help with depression, trauma, health issues, and more.

But, alas, my family did not have lengthy discussions about divorce. As it turned out, divorce was granted the same respect and attention as pregnancy: it was avoided at all costs. Betty was not happy that my divorce had hit the papers in two states. I never saw the stories, but I trusted that she had them clipped and saved, just in case.

When the time came near for John 2.0 to head out to his next duty station, he asked me to go with him. "Yes, of course," I said. The summer of hanging out, loving, and feeling loved was good medicine for me, and the thought of getting out of town, far from the people and things that caused me pain, was more than appealing.

John left first, and I spent a few months settling everything at home and spending time with my family. He came back to get me in November 1982. We married and headed to Fort Polk, Louisiana, in his Jeep Scrambler, towing my 1976 brown Ford Mustang filled with my belongings and a cat named Hooter.

THE DEATH OF A HONEYMOON

I could not wait to meet all my new hubby's Army buddies, and their girlfriends and wives, who were waiting for us there. John had told me about them all summer and on our long drive from Northern Kentucky to the Louisiana–Texas border. We pulled up at our tiny home off base, dropped off my car, cat, and U-Haul, jumped back in his Jeep Scrambler, and headed to base to meet the gang.

It was the weekend, so I hoped they were expecting us. Most everyone should be there. A mini wedding reception is what I had imagined. But the base seemed like a ghost town when we arrived. A mangled vehicle sat at the front of the company barracks. John left me in the Jeep and went to find his lieutenant.

The night before last, the lieutenant explained, six of the soldiers had piled into a car and gone out on the town. On the way home, the driver had fallen asleep, and the car had run off a steep embankment into a tree, killing all but two of the passengers. One would be okay, but the other was in a coma. The only soldier in the vehicle who had not been drinking had been sitting in the middle of the back seat when the drive shaft impaled him while he had slept.

John was crushed. His friends were gone. They may have been celebrating our wedding that night when the driver had fallen asleep at the wheel and soared midair into the tree. John and I drove to the place where the accident had occurred. I was astonished that anyone had survived. The fall to the ground from where the car hit the tree was maybe 40 feet.

I recalled the terrifying accident that had happened in my hometown a few years prior. A teen driving fast down Highway 16 lost control, striking a telephone pole at 50-plus miles per hour. He was killed instantly, but first responders never assume—someone had to climb in that vehicle and check. Because the car was mangled, the door would not open quickly. My mom was on that ambulance call and, being the smallest, she climbed through the broken window to check the young man for a pulse. There was none. The jaws of life eventually freed the victim, and the ambulance headed off to the hospital.

My mother came home later, walked into the shower with her clothes on, and did not come out for an hour. She said it was horrifying to watch his blood wash down the shower drain. It would be many more showers before she felt she no longer had his blood on herself.

John and I left the scene at the tree and quietly went home. The shadow of that event changed our relationship immediately and forever. He was never quite the same again; he never seemed to enjoy another night out. And his mental anguish became my mental anguish as well. He was distraught but sought no help. He was angry, and he was not sure where to direct that anger. He was, by all accounts, grieving.

John 2.0 started keeping tight reins on me and did so for the remainder of our ten-year marriage. Sometimes he timed me when I left the house—including visits to the grocery store. He scared me once when I was shopping at the IGA near our home. I guess I had been gone longer than he expected, so he drove to the store and walked around until he found me. But he waited in the next aisle. When I turned the corner and saw him standing there, waiting for me, I nearly fainted. I pushed our boys and the groceries to the checkout and got the heck out of there. To this day, I seriously hate grocery shopping. I guess I always have. But thank goodness for home delivery.

I had no idea at the time that John was most probably suffering from PTSD, depression, or at the very least, grief, from the loss of his friends. We never discussed his pain. It was years later, during my recovery process, that I realized the distress this man must have been dealing with and how it had reflected in our relationship and others. I wish I could go back and give him the love and support he needed.

In Louisiana, I sold my Mustang that I had saved up to purchase, and my clarinet that I had loved since sixth grade. We needed the money—but these losses added to my sadness.

There I was, just a kid with no local friends. No close family. No assistance for off-base spouses. Very few possessions. And 875 miles from home. John needed help and I needed help, and we were too young to see it. I began to resent him.

I moved out, with plans to get back home and file for divorce. Getting a divorce in Louisiana was, at the very least, difficult. I started a relationship with another man and did my best to make 2.0 hate me and leave me alone. He did not, and somehow, we worked out some of the grief and reconciled, agreeing to try to make the marriage work.

John 2.0 and I struggled as husband and wife. We loved each other, but I never felt that our relationship fully recovered after his Army buddies' wreck. He was overly demanding, and I was resentful and headstrong, but we were determined to make a go of it anyway.

A new love blossomed when we discovered I was pregnant with our first child. We made plans to leave the Army and head home sometime after the baby was born. It was exciting to get back home to Northern Kentucky and start over again.

During the next few years of a tumultuous marriage, and in between the separations, we were either happily in love or at odds with each other. One evening after picking up our son Jacob from daycare, I arrived home to find John burning a big barrel of something in the front yard of our little farmhouse.

After years of this unpredictable type of behavior, I guess I had become numb—call it the first sign of Stockholm syndrome. I looked in the barrel and saw my childhood toys, dolls, diaries, pictures, clothes, coveted books, and personal items burning in there. I believe my comment to him was an emotionless "huh." I turned as if I had seen nothing burning in the barrel and took my baby and my groceries into the house. I would not give John the satisfaction of seeing me sad. But little pieces of my heart were breaking off and floating away in the smoke.

I can picture the contents of that barrel—even now. Etched into my brain are the embers of pages of Tracy's gifted Trixie Belden books and the melted body of a ballerina that once turned atop my now-charred pink jewelry box. But to this day, I still cannot remember why he was angry at me. I am sure it was one of those "at odds" times of our marriage.

Sadly, we would separate and reconcile again and again, hurting each other deeper with each round, until one terrible fight in the early 1990s that would end the marriage for good.

CONGRATULATIONS, YOU ARE PREGNANT
WITH A SIDE DISH OF DYSPLASIA

Somewhere in between all the separations, there was a time of bliss. John, little seven-month-old Jacob, and I had returned to Northern Kentucky in August 1984 and eventually started attending church regularly; John and I both volunteered as youth ministers. I worked in music with the little ones, and John assisted with the teens. We loved our little Jacob.

I was working at a local law firm as a paralegal, and John was finishing his degree in education and technology. A part of me was envious of his ability to drop everything and go back to college. But I was still in the self-loathing "Sylvia Must Be Punished" mode, so I accepted that I should work full-time, and he should get a degree.

I managed evening classes in journalism from Cincinnati Bible Seminary and a certification in Advanced Paralegal Studies from the Kentucky Trial Attorneys Association, but the juris doctorate degree seemed far out of reach.

After the second missed period and the blue line appeared on the test strip, I made an appointment with a gynecologist. "You are definitely pregnant," Dr. Lavender announced the obvious. Due in mid-November 1987. He would call when my other test results came back in. The tests came back, and the doctor's nurse called me.

"Mrs. 2.0, this is Hazel from Dr. Lavender's office. Your tests are in, and the doctor would like you to come to the office to discuss the results right away. Is today good for you?"

I immediately pushed back. "Can we go over this on the phone? I cannot miss a lot of work right now."

"No," Hazel insisted. "This is urgent."

Hazel and I would volley back and forth until I had sufficient information about my condition. Third-stage advanced dysplasia, a.k.a. early cervical cancer.

My immediate visit to Dr. Lavender would ease my mind but didn't change the diagnosis. Advanced precancerous cells covered the cervix and were growing. If they moved to the vaginal wall as expected, the prognosis was grim considering the pregnancy.

"The procedure that needs to be done immediately will be dangerous for the baby and most likely cause the baby to abort," Doc said. "But, without this, it will continue to spread." The options were obvious and ugly: (1) undergo a cone biopsy, (2) undergo an abortion followed by a full hysterectomy, or (3) do nothing.

Dr. Lavender was a godly man, and he encouraged me to get a second opinion or even transfer to another ob-gyn. He could not and would not encourage abortion per his own personal beliefs but would not be offended if I grabbed my file and went elsewhere. He handed me my folder and awaited my decision.

Suddenly, I had a second chance to make the right choice. The circumstances were different, and no one would have questioned my decision this time. I recalled Dr. Seuss's last line in *Horton*:

"From sun in the summer, From rain when it's fall-ish, I'm going to protect them. No matter how small-ish!"

"You know, Doc, let's just let this little baby have a chance. If you will remain my doctor during this, I'll be your patient until the end." I figured if the last thing I did was to give birth to this little person, then that is what would happen. Lavender had me revisit the office monthly for a look-see at the cervix and the baby, and the growth and development of both.

Hazel would load me up after each visit with pamphlets on how to deal with cancer, especially terminal cancer, cervical surgeries, and the risks, as well as how to tell others about your illness. I tossed them all in the garbage can outside the medical building on my fat, pregnant waddle back to my car.

Up to the very day Isaac was born, I worked full-time at the law firm, teetering up and down a spiral staircase 20 or 30 times a day. The attorney for whom I worked was a touchy-feely kind of guy. And I am not referring to his tender heart. He was overly friendly, abusive, and rarely saw anyone else's needs over his own.

The morning of Isaac's birth, I dropped off my files at the law firm and let the staff know Isaac was going to be a week early. The infant had decided to pull out of the birth canal, and it appeared we might be in for a difficult birth.

Instead of helping me out the door to the hospital, my boss asked if I could go over a dozen cases first. And, like the doormat I had become, I complied. After wasting a half hour going over cases while in labor, I carried the files back down the spiral staircase by myself and dropped the entire caseload on the desk of the other paralegal. "Good luck," I muttered as I stumbled up the death trap (absolutely no one offering to help) and headed out the door to the hospital. It's a darn shame my water didn't break on that staircase.

At the hospital, baby Isaac's vitals started to drop. He was clearly in distress, so we went into surgery for my second emergency C-section. I insisted on being awake, which was granted. I insisted on seeing as much of the birth as a large mirror in the room would allow. Granted. I requested the doc follow the dotted line from my first C-section rather than find a new way in. Granted. When you are facing the possibility of dying, they will grant just about anything. Why didn't I ask for a string quartet to play during the surgery?

Isaac was a big baby—over nine pounds—too big for my small body. But a happy, healthy, and sweet baby. Jacob was immediately in love with his new little brother and insisted on holding him all the time. John was elated and proud of son number two. And I was sent home with another set of staples in my abdomen and a child who, I was told, would be my last.

Lavender's plan was for me to recover from the C-section. Once the staples were out, I was scheduled to go back into surgery immediately. Isaac had developed erythema toxicum (an itchy red rash) shortly after birth, and rather than clearing up right away as expected, it continued to spread across his little body.

As we discovered later, Isaac had allergies—to everything. He was allergic to, well, Earth. The whole planet. But for an itchy, scratchy little baby, he was really happy. Whether he was waking from a nap or just nursing, he would look right in my eyes. I'd wonder, what are you thinking about, little man?

It was a joyful time without my multiple caseloads from work and with two little boys I loved more than anyone else on the planet. I thought I might be spending the last days of my life with my babies.

Two days after I arrived home with my new baby, my boss showed up at my door with two boxes of cases. "Can you work on these when the baby is sleeping," he sort of asked, but really didn't expect an answer. Now, I should have punched him. But, no, I said, "Sure."

SOMEBODY MISPLACED MY DYSPLASIA

Several weeks later, I arrived at the surgery center around 5 a.m. Dad was with me. I would be sedated. I would go through a full exam of my infected cervix, confirming the spreading cancer, and then my entire female reproductive system would be removed. I would remain at the hospital for tests and recovery for an unknown number of days.

After surgery, there would be more tests to determine whether and where the cancer might have spread during the pregnancy. And I would be given options for treatment.

Dad was there when I woke from a strange dream. I tried to tell him about the dream. But he was telling me that they could not FIND it. "Find what, Pop?" I slurred out.

"There was nothing there," he continued. "It's gone!"

My mind was blurry, and the drugs they had used to put me under were still working rather well, but I was certain he meant they took out the uterus, tubes, and the infected cervix. But that was not what he was trying to tell me.

A GOOD TRADE

One Sunday morning about a month before Isaac was born, most of the congregation of Nicholson Christian Church came over to where I sat, some laying hands on my shoulders, back, and arms, others standing near, but everyone praying for baby Isaac and me and our little family. James 5:14 NIV: "Is anyone among you sick?" We were praying in Faith for healing and forgiveness.

At my six-month prenatal checkup, I convinced the doc to allow me to volunteer at Camp Northward as a counselor. I planned to take my big pregnant belly and my sweet little three-year-old Jacob and stay a week in a cabin in the woods far from home with a bunch of nine- and ten-year-old kids. How better to spend my one-week-a-year vacation.

As a child, I spent every summer at Camp Northward in Pendleton County, Kentucky. Without cell phones or social media, my Christian summer camp friends found each other every year from the age of eight until sixteen. I was saved at church camp, got my first kiss at church camp—thanks to Kevin Kerns—and learned the value of good friends and good memories. It had been a dream to go back and give back. But if I did not go now, I may never have a chance. Granted.

Stranger things have happened, I have been told. And Dr. Lavender was as baffled as a doctor might be—a doctor who had just spent the last eight months telling you that your chances were grim. But now? Right out of surgery, he was almost apologizing.

"We did the initial exam." The doc held his hands clasped in his lap as he spoke. "But the cervix was clean and clear without a blemish. Nothing was there!"

I did not know how to feel. Was it a miracle? God does heal. Prayer does work. But was there some reason God would spare me when I had been such a loser in the past? After all, I hadn't saved my dust speck.

Weirdly and only briefly, I felt as cheated as Dr. Lavender felt embarrassed and baffled. I had planned for the worst for months, and now it was just… gone. Dr. Lavender, my dad, and I sat there, befuddled, and we prayed.

Over the years, Isaac and I have discussed this event. He was my little miracle baby whom I refused to abort. In return, Isaac teases me that he cleared up my cancer and took it out of the womb with him in the form of a rash. Good trade, we both agree, pounding our chests in some made-up tribal ritual we adapted from *Dances with Wolves*. But Dr. Lavender and our family did agree that it was truly a miracle, and we may never know exactly how or why God pulled it off.

If not God, then how? Was there something I was doing or had done that reversed the cancer? I've read a ton of stories, medical studies, and theories on the subject, but the book that caught my eye was *The War of Art: Break Through the Blocks and Win Your Inner Creative Battles* by Steven Pressfield.

Pressfield documented stories of people given the news of terminal cancer who turned immediately from what they *were* doing to what they had always *dreamed* of doing—their *calling*, if you will. Seeking out their true talent—finding the one thing they were supposed to do on this planet and getting busy doing it before it was too late!

According to Pressfield, somewhere in the transformation from wrong path to right path, the cancer went into remission or disappeared altogether. People given only months to live lived many years into the future. Was my decision to not abort Isaac and do what was right in my mind part of my cure?

Was giving back to the church through volunteering—something I had always wanted to do—part of my cure? I do not know. I know that my focus was on being happy, staying healthy for the baby, helping others anyway I could, and having hope in God that Isaac would make it full term. Was "happy" a cure? Isaac does mean "laughter" after all.

Maybe the simple answer is that I was not demanding to be healed. I wasn't even thinking about being healed. I was simply living, loving, helping, and trusting that God would take me home in His time. Psalm 23:1,4 NIV: "[1]The Lord is my Shepherd, I lack nothing." [4] "Even though I walk through the darkest valley, I will fear no evil, for you are with me." I am giving God the glory on this one. And so did Dr. Lavender. And so should you. My guardian angel was grinning from ear to ear as he worked his way forward from the back of the throne room.

THERE'S ALWAYS WOMB FOR ONE MOORE

In 1993, I opened a title search company. I had suffered through my share of workplace sexual harassment from Louisiana to Kentucky to Georgia and had decided perhaps legal research was best done without horny attorneys or rich clients chasing me about the law libraries.

The secrets I was asked to keep for these men through the years bother me still today. These men didn't earn nor deserve my protection. But I needed my jobs. Pushing off constant advances became a true talent for me. I was a "Dolly Parton '9 to 5'" survivor for years. There should be a freaking award for putting up with that crud.

Back in high school, I was shocked and caught off-guard by a teacher who decided pushing me back onto a desk and groping me was okay. I hated that man after that, but I never shared the assault with a soul. One night at dinner, my mother, the mayor, mentioned her distaste for this teacher. "Same here, Mom," I added as we ate her famous fried chicken. She was surprised at my comment because this teacher was beloved by most students. But she never asked me for more information—and I never offered more. We simply understood each other on that subject.

When I left Louisiana in 1984, I thought I had left the employer sexual harassment behind me. But I landed an awesome paralegal position with a Kentucky firm and discovered quickly that the attorney I worked for had a long reputation of infidelity. He kept photos of his successful campaigns, which I found one day while reorganizing the file room.

When we moved to Georgia, I worked for a great firm. The attorneys were great, but a few of their wealthier clients were insulting and forward, and I finally had enough.

I went out on my own for the first time. I was calling the shots now, and I decided on the firms for which I would work. My first client was a female attorney. How refreshing.

Shortly after 2.0 and I divorced in 1993, he decided he would pack up a U-Haul, resign from his job, and move back to Kentucky to start over.

James was a quiet and kind man who worked at the county courthouse, where most of my research took place. We started a friendship that eventually blossomed. He was everything the other men in my life were not, plus all the good qualities combined: honest, kind, quiet, handsome, and trustworthy.

We never fought. It was a peaceful, quiet marriage that I certainly did not feel I deserved.

Before our marriage, I had been suffering from Stockholm syndrome because of my previous marriage. Tight restraints, never alone, and fights—all the time, about everything—had left me a bit damaged.

It took several years before I could walk through a grocery store without checking the time and feeling afraid to turn the aisle. The idea of going to the mall alone was unthinkable. I would break out in a sweat just considering it. To this day, I hate the mall. I can count on one hand the number of times I have been to the mall in the last 30 years. Thank goodness for online shopping.

It is baffling now to think that I never knew I had trauma-related problems. I didn't notice because it had slowly become a normal part of life for me. I went from cocoon to butterfly, and then butterfly to caterpillar to cocoon, a mixed-up metamorphosis, and I didn't even notice.

I was also the frog in the lukewarm water with the heat going up and up. But this is a proven myth that the frog does not notice. The truth is, when the water gets too hot, the frog always jumps out. So did I. Hard cold fact is that I should have never placed myself in the pot of lukewarm water in the first place.

After James and I married, we were concerned that having a child was out of the question because of my past medical history. About the time we were considering getting help, I became pregnant.

The doctors were concerned. I would be at high risk, as would the baby during the entire pregnancy. I had been testing every couple of months for seven years—just waiting for the cancer to return. It did not. A cone biopsy, another couple of biopsies, years of cysts and endometriosis since Isaac's birth, the past abortion (which I lied about and told my doctor it had been a miscarriage), and the two C-sections had left my womb compromised and my cervix in poor shape and somehow tilted. It was not the best environment in which to grow a child, but more akin to trying to bake a Thanksgiving turkey in an Easy-Bake Oven. It was possible, but it was going to be messy and not without risk.

Baby Daniel tried to arrive early for months, but we always fought him back. I was enormous, and my blood pressure was off the chain. But we made it to the end, scheduling baby Daniel for my final C-section in February 1996.

Once again, I was permitted to stay awake for the C-section. And after following the dotted line for the second time, there he was: baby Daniel Moore, my third little miracle baby. My fourth and last child. My doctor was proud and amazed.

"You did it, lady," said my doc.

"Yes, sir," I replied. "There's Always Womb for One Moore."

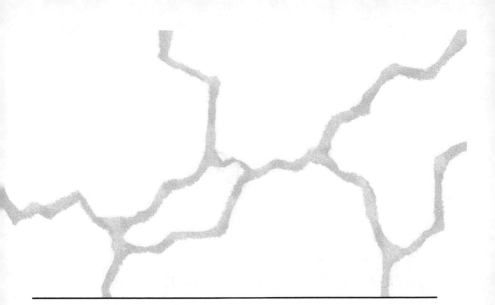

PART 2:

When the Bowl Hits the Concrete

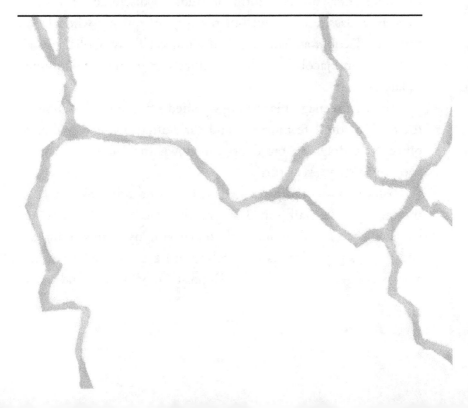

BOOB PRETZELS AND BANK DEPOSIT WARS

I t was a Friday, and Isaac reveled in the front seat of the family van. *No school today* was plastered on his grinning face. Friday morning at the dentist and permission to miss the rest of day was a great start to any 16-year-old's weekend. "We *are* going by the office after your appointment kiddo," I disclosed. Isaac's face froze in a classic teen pout but thawed out quickly when I told him that Jacob was working at the office all day. College finals were over, and Jacob was full-time office staff until classes resumed in late January.

The two teenage Hardy Boys goofed off like grade-schoolers for most of the late morning and early afternoon. Five-wheeled office-chair dragsters raced up and down the hallway, breaking speed records at every turn.

Bank-deposit-stamp wars ensued, and no one was safe from the carnage. The staff joined in, and the place was in thunderous hysteria when I walked out of my office with my resting mom face and Friday's payroll in hand. Jacob's and Isaac's clothes, faces, and arms were graffitied with "For Deposit Only" in red and black, and Jacob had two fat pretzel bites stuck in his shirt suggesting, well, boobs.

"This is not a playground," I admonished in my best mom-boss voice.

My serious, straight mouth curved into a smirk when Jacob reached up inside his shirt, pulled out a pretzel, popped it in his mouth, and muttered in between crunches, "But Laura told me to do it."

The laughter that ensued was contagious, and Laura, an agent and one of my dearest friends, slinked back in one of the race chairs and shrugged. "It seemed like a good idea," she confessed.

Jacob continued to eat his boob pretzels, patted me on the back a few times, and sashayed down the hallway to his desk.

It *was* a great start to a weekend.

We drove home later—little Daniel in his booster seat and Isaac riding shotgun, planning our Friday night dinner. We were ready to have a Christmassy weekend.

Back at the office, agents had already headed home, and the staff was planning to shut down for the weekend. Jacob called just before 5 p.m. "Hey, Mom, can I cut out of here early?" He planned to cash his paycheck, grab a bite to eat, and head to his friend John's house to play guitar.

"Sure," I conceded. "Will you stay the night or head home?"

Jacob and James had recently had a heart-to-heart discussion about Jacob's late nights at friends' houses and his coming home after midnight on school nights, and how that was unfair to his younger brothers. Jacob had agreed to earlier weekdays and quieter entries on the weekends, and in return, we would move Isaac in with Daniel and give Jacob back his own bedroom over the weekend.

At 19, Jacob attended college full time with a recently received scholarship at Middle Georgia State University. He had a sweet girlfriend, Jenny, and he was a talented musician. His life was learning, dating, working, and playing guitar. Life was simple.

"Jenny doesn't get off until after midnight. She wants to drop by on her way home, so I'll probably stay at John's," Jacob replied.

"Okey-doke, just be home early so we can have breakfast and finish the tree," I said. Jacob and I were the only family members who enjoyed decorating the Christmas tree. We often made ornaments for it; this year had been no exception—glass globe ornaments hand-painted with acrylics in mosaic patterns.

"Absolutely. See ya in the morning."

"See ya then. I love you. Have fun."

"Love you too, Mom. See ya tomorrow."

"Bye."

"Bye."

That was the last conversation we had that Friday. I would not see him again until the next morning.

CLUES AND LESSONS

On any given weekday morning, I would watch the news. This early Friday morning, I was already dressed, waiting for Isaac to finish breakfast and brush his teeth. "Why do I have to brush my teeth if I am having my teeth cleaned?" Isaac argued.

"Brush your teeth anyway," I demanded. We had plenty of time since his appointment was an hour away, so I was flipping through the cable channels, thoughtlessly wasting time.

I stopped to catch the QVC network showing off the newest Tiffany-inspired floor lamp, and I made a mental note to buy that lamp someday. Then, a commercial for PlayStation's *The Getaway* caught my attention for a few seconds, and I made a mental note to never buy that game for my boys.

A talk show stopped me in my tracks. My heart ached for a young couple as they discussed the details leading up to their daughter's death from terminal cancer. "We were told we would get over it," the mother recalled. "Time will heal, they said."

"Yes, like our beautiful little girl was going to be a memory that fades over time," the father of the six-year-old added.

If losing her was not bad enough, the horrible advice family and friends gave afterward was like salt in an open wound: God needed another angel, they would have more children, they were lucky to have her for even a brief time, and she was a loan from God.

Why do people blame God for every death? God does not check people in and out of our lives like a librarian. And we should spare the "God of Wrath and Love" chat with a parent who lost a child and think instead about poor Mary standing there at the cross. She knew her child was dying, and I am certain she knew why, yet she cried and wept and mourned as he died. She was horrified by Jesus' death. Sickened by His suffering. In utter and total despair, she wept. Her grief was amplified by the fact that she stood helpless as He died. There was nothing she could do to stop it.

"People were wrong," the young mother revealed. "Our daughter is not gone. She is a goal. We will not get *over* the loss of our daughter. She will always be in our hearts. And someday we want to be where she is."

The two young parents revealed something that I would discover was key to survival in this world: hope. And not just hope, but the path to healing and creating healthy habits that lead to happiness. The message was there—just not completely articulated. When the world gets completely off balance, where do we muster the courage and strength to face the unthinkable? Why do children have to suffer? How can we feel normal again? Is there such a thing as normal?

I would discover this recipe as I sifted through the nightmare heading my way later that evening and into Saturday morning. I would learn that for me and my family to be happy again, we would need to create habits that practice and share happiness. Begin healing by forgiving, giving, and incorporating healthy living, eating, and thinking. To feel whole again, we must embrace God's love, forgiveness, and holiness. To receive, we must be willing to give.

"We know we will see her again someday, and that is a way that we find joy, peace, and happiness," the couple shared as the show came to an end. Their book could be purchased by calling a number on the screen, and I made a mental note to look for that book later as I turned off the TV and yelled for Isaac to get his butt in the van. We were officially late for the dentist. From the dentist to the office, from boob pretzels to Friday-night popcorn, the night was as normal as the day had been.

THE CALL

The beep of the answering machine woke us, and a woman began to speak. "James, Sylvia?" It was James's mom, a.k.a. Grandma Judy. She sounded shaken and anxious. By this time, we were both walking for the phone and looking at the time and at each other. She told us we had missed a call from a hospital in Macon. There was indeed another message on the machine before hers—a man from the emergency room asking us to call immediately.

After my brother Bo had died earlier that year, I'd made each of the boys a little laminated card for their wallets or book bags that listed everyone in the family plus phone numbers. The hospital had begun calling from top to bottom on this chilly Saturday morning in December. Grandma Judy was the first to answer the call we had missed.

Macon, Georgia, is about 25 to 30 minutes from our town. It seemed odd and frightening that someone would be calling us from Macon. But my sinking heart already knew it must be about Jacob. His brothers were fast asleep. The local hospital was only about 10 minutes away in traffic. *Why was Jacob in Macon?* I asked myself. The hairs on my arms began to rise with prickling pain.

I dialed the number immediately, and the same man answered the phone. "Are you Jacob's mother?" He told me Jacob was injured, and I needed to come to the hospital immediately.

"Is he okay? Was he in an accident?" I asked.

Silent for a second, the man then replied, "Please come right away."

"I'm sorry," I implored, "I need to know. What happened? Are we too late?"

He was gentle but firm in his reply: "I'm sorry, I am not allowed to say anything over the phone, but I can tell you that he is injured, and you need to drive here right now—please!"

We were already dressing quickly in yesterday's clothes found atop the laundry basket as we spoke to the man. We jumped in the car and called Judy to come to the house and watch the boys. James was driving as if on the autobahn, passing cars, trucks, and RVs on the expressway, with lights flashing. We knew this was going to be more than just serious. We felt it. Shock and numbness wrestled in my brain. I needed to call his dad, and Jenny's mom, Dawn.

I called John on the way to the hospital. He answered right away. I don't know how I knew; I guess it was all the factors put together—the questions I'd asked and how the man had answered or not answered—but I thought maybe Jacob had been shot. It was an accident, but not a wreck? I didn't really know. There was no explanation. We just had to hurry.

The Hardy family dressed quickly and started the long drive from Northern Kentucky to Middle Georgia. Jacob's dad would tell me later that he had felt like something was wrong that evening when he'd gone to bed. Was it a parental connection? A whisper from God? Does God do that?

We learned later that Jacob had purchased a Mountain Dew and a Snickers bar in a gas station and had just reentered his 1990 Ford truck when a four-door sedan pulled up beside him. A man jumped out, stood at Jacob's window, and asked for a light. Jacob's passenger complied, and when Jacob turned back to the window to hand over a lighter, the man attacked our son.

We called Jenny's mom on the way to the hospital. "Hey, Dawn, is Jenny home?" James asked.

"Yeah, uh, I think so, yeah." Dawn hesitated but was certain in her final answer. It was late. We gave Dawn the news that Jacob was injured, we had no details, but we were on the way to Macon. She woke Jenny from her last good night's sleep for a long while.

Running into the hospital emergency center, I was met by the trauma team, and they led me quickly to Jacob's side. Now the words that came out of their mouths and into my head and my heart were spears—each word piercing a new part of my heart, brain, and soul.

Jacob had been shot in the head. It will be shocking to see, they warned. He may not survive. The bullet shot completely through his brain. But right now, he is alive. James stepped outside to call Grandma Judy to bring the boys right away. I walked in to see my son.

I saw him, but there were no words. I spoke to him, but without a voice. I looked into his big green eyes, but there was no clarity. No reason. I walked in to see my son dying on a hospital gurney. His head was a mess, with blood, brain matter, and God knows what else lying around him on the gurney.

Why was no one treating him? Where were the surgeons? Why weren't we preparing him for ... something, anything? Was he a lost cause? I was standing there as helpless as Mary. My son was dying. But I did NOT know why. And there was nothing I could do to stop it.

At that very moment, nothing mattered to me. Nothing but that boy lying there. That 19-year-old, nearly-six-foot-tall baby of mine. The funny little baby who laughed and chatted about everything. Taught himself sign language as a young child so he could talk to one of his best friends, John, who had lost his hearing from meningitis. Taught himself to play guitar. Was studying coding and business at the same time. Hated baseball but loved alternative rock. This little boy.

What the heck, Jacob? What were you doing? How did this happen? Wake up and tell me what happened. I didn't know it, but it was my brain that was breaking, not just my heart. We always blame it on the heart. But distress, trauma, loss, and pain are experienced in the brain, and it sends shock waves to the rest of the body. It is also the brain that gives us the ability to deal with trauma. We will discuss that later.

Within 24 hours, I would find courage and a reason to hope. In all this insanity, I would find the path back to happiness. Although I wanted to curl up and die right beside my child, I would be healthy again. Not by forgetting, getting past it, or putting anything behind me. No, I would carry this loss with me along the way. So will you. And that is perfectly fine.

WHEN NOTHING MAKES SENSE

The horrible details started to filter through the mouths of investigators and eyewitnesses that early Saturday morning of December 6th.

Before Jacob was shot, he was tortured with blinding pepper spray—police grade. Jacob screamed and fought to see. He tried to start his truck and get away. As he fumbled for his ignition, the killer reached inside the truck and shot Jacob below the ear.

The bullet traveled through the back of his brain and out the other side, skimming over the back of the teen sitting beside him, punching through the glass truck window, and then traveling some 100 yards across a field, through a metal building, bouncing off the wall on the other side, and hitting the concrete floor, where it was recovered by a detective and still resides in an envelope at the DA's office.

Jacob's face hit the steering wheel.

The attacker fled with his three accomplices. An off-duty police officer had been filling his gas tank when the shot was fired. He ran to the truck and opened the door, and Jacob slumped into his arms and onto the ground. The officer called for help and began to treat Jacob as the attacker sped out of the parking lot.

The nurse broke my silence. "Are there other family members coming in?" she politely asked.

"Um, yes, all of them." My words felt as if they were coming from somewhere other than my body. A stranger inside of me tried to make sense of this. No one could see him this way, I thought. "Can we clean him up a bit?" I asked.

"My thoughts exactly," she said. "Can you step outside for a minute?" She already knew my answer.

"No, I can't. But I can help you."

I was ready to defend my ground with years of first-responder experience, but instead we worked together to add bandages, clean the gurney, and prepare Jacob for visitors. His face was cleaner, his wounds more concealed. He looked almost like he might pull through. Almost.

Jacob's green eyes were wide open and, from what I had been told, the pressure from his swelling brain was forcing them to stay open. To this day I regret not adding drops to his eyes. I'm sure the nurses did that, but it still bothers me. His attacker used police-grade pepper spray or some other spray from the pits of Hell. It was sickening to me that Jacob suffered. And, if he had survived, he could most likely be blind.

His heart was beating, air was going in and out of his lungs, and he was reactive to touch—tickling his foot would cause a slight knee jerk, and squeezing his hand might cause him to squeeze back.

For all intents and purposes to the onlooker, it appeared that he would survive. But after several brain scans, the doctors assured me there was no brain activity. The bullet took with it a good deal of the cerebellum, and scrambled parts of the temporal and occipital lobes. Eventually, and quickly, his body would shut down completely.

THE HEART DOES GO ON

She approached with a soft smile of love and understanding. While her name now eludes me, I remember her face. She introduced herself as well as her organization, LifeLink. I'm not sure how she worded this without totally ticking me off, but she did. I heard the sincerity in her voice as she explained how Jacob had signed an organ donor card. And, while she had every hope that Jacob would make it through this ordeal, the hospital only calls her when it seems unlikely the victim will recover.

At 16, Jacob had spoken to both John and James about the back of his driver's license. Agreeing it was an awesome thing to do, he signed the card. Now at 19, with a fatal head injury, his other organs were up for grabs, and they wanted us to agree to the donation before Jacob's body shut down. They also wanted him on total life support to keep his organs in good shape.

Five families were waiting to hear. Five people could have a new chance for life today, with Jacob's organs. Five men and women would hold their children or grandchildren again. Hundreds, if not thousands, would have a chance at a new, longer life from his gifts of tissue. Nothing above the shoulders, not his beautiful green eyes, because the murder investigation warranted an autopsy.

But by the end of that first Saturday, the 6th of December, a new chance at life would be gifted by our son. There was no high fiving at this event. We were glad. Not excited. But it would give us joy later. To be healed, you must be willing to give. Healing begins with Helping.

We never regretted the decision to help others. We have never met the five who lived on. But I have kept up with their progress over the years. All but one of the major organ recipients has passed. It's sad to lose these people whom I never met. They took a piece of Jacob with them on their journey through life. I hope they get to chat with him in Heaven.

The hospital filled with hundreds of people, teens, their parents, friends—everyone wanting to see Jacob, in case it was their love that would bring him back. Balloons, flowers, and cards rolled into the area just outside the ICU. Every face, sad or hopeful or mortified. Dawn and Jenny arrived. The Hardy family would arrive shortly thereafter.

FOR DEPOSIT ONLY

Once cleaned up, Jacob was placed in ICU awaiting the final brain-activity tests and a final decision from the four parents on organ donation. And although the decision was unanimous, it was not a great comfort.

The three pastors from our churches stood beside us in the ICU. Daniel and Isaac stood over their brother; Jenny held his hand. We were saying our last goodbyes.

"Mom." Isaac was smiling through his tears. "Look," he said as he pointed to Jacob's arm and back to his own arm. Jacob's and Isaac's arms bore the red and black "For Deposit Only" marks from the stamp wars the day before. We all smiled and then chuckled slightly at each other. It was a happy memory. Right there in the ICU.

Isaac also revealed that there were bank stamps on the back of the brown sweater I had worn all day and thrown back on before heading to the hospital. It seemed Jacob had been doing more than patting me on the back at the office—I too was a target of the "For Deposit Only" stamp wars. It was strange, but we were happy about that.

That little nugget that brought a brief smile was like a falling star, and stardust gently softened this horrible event. It is the small smiles that can save a broken heart.

Grandma Judy vacuum-sealed that sweater for me, along with a couple of Jacob's smelly t-shirts. I look at the sweater from time to time to remember the little gifts God gave us to get us through that day and the heartache that would last for many years. Until the smell wore off, I would pull out the T-shirts on occasion and remember how Jacob and his favorite cologne smelled – Polo Blue I think. These were a few of the falling stars and sprinkles of stardust we saw during this horrible winter storm.

I had a choice to be happy about the things that were happy. Bank stamps we shared that day. Boob pretzels. Bittersweet. But there was hope hiding in the mess before me, and I allowed myself to see it and hang on to it. Healing takes courage.

The brain is a funky mess of gray stuff. But it heals, remembers, and compiles data, and it is in the brain that we feel love and loss. We blame the heart. You know, broken hearts and all that jazz. But it is our brain that is broken when we suffer from a broken heart, a lost love, or the death of a child, spouse, or parent. The brain tells the heart, and the heart bears the hurt.

After the final brain scan, it was confirmed that Jacob was truly gone. Everyone cried unceasingly, surrounded by friends and family as we learned and shared the news that Jacob was already gone. I don't think the kids stopped crying for days. I'm pretty sure it was days for all of us. But, when the truth about brain scan sunk in, I realized Jacob had died in the parking lot in the arms of a stranger, and I was not there when he'd headed to Heaven.

As each family member said goodbye and left the room, it was just me and the preacher trio standing over my boy. It was time for a final prayer before we left the hospital staff to prepare Jacob for his final act. Then it hit me!

"Wait." I was choked up, and the word came out as a whisper. "I have to tell you a story." I shared the details from the morning TV show with the young parents and their thoughts about their little girl. "Jacob's not gone, he's a goal," I announced. "I know where he is. I want to be where he is now. Hope is not gone; hope is in Heaven." I believe I saw stardust falling from Heaven at that very moment. I had picked up a falling star that morning and put it in my pocket, and now it was dusting the ICU.

There were no dry eyes in the ICU. God had given me a gift that morning. A little clarity. He gave me some comfort to carry me through my loss of that day and into the days that would come. He gave me courage, hope, and a way to healing and happiness. He reminded me that He had never left me. I was going to learn to create habits that would lead my family and me to heal. We would laugh again. We could feel normal again. And I saw it. "I had walked through darkness, faced death, but I was not afraid. God was there the whole time." Psalm 23, Sylvia Myers Version.

There, in the middle of my loss, grief, and trauma, I saw a little sprinkle of hope, the possibility for happiness, and even holiness on the horizon. My biggest challenge was how to pick up all the broken pieces of my heart and find the path to healing.

PICKING OUT A COFFIN

This is one of the hardest parts for most parents. There is no right or wrong choice. And it was really freaking hard. It took strength or stupidity or a combination of both. Maybe we were just too numb. Or we just knew it was the right thing to do.

But, for a person to become an organ donor and benefit the most people, the organs must still be working right up to the minute before harvested for another human being.

This meant that in no way would we have days to linger at the hospital. There would be no holding Jacob while he passed away in my arms. We would not watch the monitors beep, beep … beep … … … … beep … … … … … into silence.

As a matter of fact, this meant walking away from a warm, breathing child, with his heart beating, his skin reactive to the touch, knowing that the next time I saw him he would be cold, dead in a coffin of our choosing, as if this terror could get any worse.

We left the hospital, headed home, and prepared to head back out later that morning to choose a coffin for a child who was still warm and in surgery. They were slicing him up for evidence and pulling out parts to fly all over the country in small coolers. I did not see the event. But I pictured it in great and horrific detail.

We would all sleep—but only for a couple of hours. The horrifying first morning after the death of a child, brother, lover, or grandchild is like a bad dream that turns out to be true. You Scream. Loudly. And then you Scream again.

As we drove to the funeral parlor, I could only picture the surgeons cutting into my son to get his lungs, kidneys, liver—everything they needed or wanted. This was horrifying. This was not a comfort, and there was no stardust falling. I did not care about the people receiving his organs. Not yet. Not then. I was angry. Not at his killer. I didn't think about that young man either. Heck, the police were still looking for him for days after Jacob's death. I was angry that Jacob was gone. I was angry he had suffered. I was angry.

I was haunted by the pitiful memory of losing my first unborn baby, and it came banging into my brain saying, *You don't deserve children, you loser.* This must be my punishment, I concluded. What chance do Daniel and Isaac have with a mom like me? Had I always been a bad mother? I remembered the day Jacob was born. It had been in a hospital like this one.

They handed me Jacob in the newly built Fort Baine, Louisiana, United States Army Training Hospital early in the morning on January 24, 1984, as I was just waking from emergency C-section surgery. Jacob was not only breech but facing the wrong way. His head was aiming up instead of down during labor, and his legs were folded straight up and crossed at his chest. I teased him in his teen years that he was ass-backward and upside down plus two weeks late when he was born.

It was a tough pregnancy overall, and my blood pressure had remained high during the last trimester. Jacob truly was late—due on the 4th of January. We went to bed on the 23rd wondering if there would be a baby anytime soon.

The doctors didn't seem too concerned about the delay or my blood pressure. But that changed as they prepared me for emergency surgery. Jacob was indeed going the wrong way, and he was in trouble.

The room filled with excited young doctors in training as someone stuck a long, painful needle in my back. "Everyone will please BE QUIET UNTIL THE PAIN STOPS," I demanded to the noisy room as the labor pain shot through my body. And just like that, the room full of Army officers was silent, the only noise coming from a cartoon playing on the corner television—invisible to the crowd until that moment when it gained full attention. Someone reached up and turned off the TV and all eyes turned back to me. I was quickly sedated and headed off to be the main show for this eager group of young docs.

When I woke up, I was greeted by an old Army nurse holding my baby over my body. "You should try to feed him right away," she demanded. John reminded me about rank in the Army and I reminded him that I was not in the Army, and I didn't like this old hag and didn't care if she was a captain, colonel, or commander in chief—she wasn't touching my boobs one more time for "proper latch for lactation." I snarled at her when she walked back in the room.

I was scared. Not of Nurse Ratchet. I was scared I would break Jacob or drop him. I was still numb from my boobs to my toes. He would certainly die of starvation, as I apparently had no clue how to breastfeed. With our families nearly a thousand miles away, we were ill prepared to be parents. We bought a baby bed, diapers and a few bottles, but never gave formula a thought.

The hospital staff was crazy for handing a little tiny baby to a barely 22-year-old. Somehow, they trusted me to care for this tiny creature. I worried how I would change him and comb his hair.

When I was six, I just tore off my dolls' heads to give them a proper hair-brushing and a fresh change of clothes. This was not going to work now. Yep, I'm going to break him, and they can see my incompetence. Yet they sent me home anyway with a brand-new baby and 16 staples in my belly.

Luckily for Jacob, all the training from being raised six down and five up in a family of ten kids kicked in, and Jacob was a healthy and happy, bottle-fed little baby. He laughed and giggled. Talked early. Walked on his first birthday. Potty-trained himself out of disgust for dirty diapers. Thankfully, learned to comb his own hair. And he held my hand when we drove anywhere. I always thought he would pick out my coffin—not the other way around.

We picked out an all-wood coffin, and four green widemouth bass for each corner of it. Jacob was an avid fisherman like his dad, so "rustic wood with fish" seemed the appropriate box design to house his remains, a pair of jeans, a Corona T-shirt he'd bought himself on vacation, and a brand-new orange American Eagle shirt we found hanging in his closet.

Later, after Jacob was tucked in his coffin, Isaac told us of the shirt snafu. Falling-star time. "Uh, Mom? You know that shirt you put on Jacob? It was my new American Eagle." We laughed. Did you hear that? We Laughed.

We recalled how the boys always borrowed each other's clothes, and we were quite sure Jacob wasn't bringing that shirt back any-time soon. Jacob was laughing with the grandparents about Isaac's shirt right now, we teased each other.

We wondered about burying him without shoes. Why dress him in shoes if no one sees them? But we should have given him flip-flops or something on his feet.

We took home the four green fish from the coffin, and we talk about them. Mine sits right here on my desk. It makes us happy to remember and to imagine if there is a fishing hole in Heaven, Jacob is there right now, stardust is floating down, his line thrown out, bobber gently floating up and down, and his bare feet are dangling in the living water.

THE MIDDLE EIGHT
(WHAT NOT TO SAY AT A FUNERAL)

S ongs have a bridge, or a middle eight. Theater has an inter-
mission. Football has halftime. Consider this next section
My Bridge—Middle Eight—Intermission During Halftime as
I properly expose why grievers learn to lie about how they feel in
"What Not to Say at a Funeral."

For centuries now, we have stigmatized loss, death, divorce,
heartbreak, and every other grief, and sentenced grievers to a lifetime of pretending and hiding from the truth. This jury sentence
of perceived weakness and accusations of exaggerated suffering
stifles the heartbroken to a life of avoiding recovery rather than
seeking recovery.

Jacob's funeral was planned, and family from all over the country flew in for the service. It was standing room only at the Shirley
Hills Baptist Church, with hundreds of people in attendance and
songs I had written to my children performed by friends.

The coffin sat at the front of the church, open. No scars were
visible. But there were scars. There were scars all over that congregation of friends and family members. Jacob seemed asleep. Like

he might wake up. But it was not a comfort. Until only recently, I could not visit that church without seeing the coffin up front, just below the podium.

To enhance my grief, others made me feel guilty, judged, and ashamed by my grief. I blamed God and then tried to bargain for a trip back in time. Then, I blamed myself, isolated myself, and tortured myself in my grief.

Sympathetic business associates mentioned books on getting past my grief. I worried about how weak I looked in my grief, so I simply stopped discussing my child's death. Other friends instructed that our family had needed his death to truly know the value of life. Shut the front door.

Sympathy is not empathy. And empathy is NOT telling someone you lost a friend in high school, so you know how they feel in losing their brother or lover or son. That is called *selfish stealing of another's grief.* But yet you hear those words at every funeral you attend, like they came from a Guide to Grief manual or an evil greeting card. Truth be told, there are no actual words that describe exactly what we want to say to someone who has lost someone they love.

The *New Oxford American Dictionary* defines *condolence* as "an expression of sympathy, especially on the occasion of a death." Also defined as solace, comfort, consolation, fellow feeling, understanding, empathy, compassion, pity, solicitude, concern, and support. Not really comforting, are they?

It was not a comfort that everyone had a loss or a friend of a friend who had lost a child or a brother or even a beloved dog. My world was on fire, and there was no water in sight. It would have been better for people to say nothing at all than to say anything without empathy, leaving all sympathy at the door.

We are taught that we should always say "something" at a funeral. I mean, we wait in a long line to get to the family to say … something. Right? And what do people say to the parents of a child who was murdered or died of cancer, sickness, or SIDS? How do you console or comfort a parent mourning the loss of a child who drowned or fell or died in a car wreck?

The number one, go-to answer is this: "I'm sorry for your loss." Good answer, and it should just stop there. Don't try to make up for the death or condone the death or justify the death in any way. But people don't stop after that first answer, do they? They just keep on talking, piling dry wood on a burning fire.

PRESENTNESS

First, be present and hug a lot, then shut your mouth. Yes, I mean go over there and sit with your friend and say absolutely nothing. Listen with both ears if they begin to talk and say nothing more to them than "I love you," and "I'm here." Then hush up. It's impossible to shed any good on this loss with words. Let it be what it is.

Bring food, smiles, love, and understanding, and don't stop after a few weeks. There is no recovery time for grief, just an easing of the trauma and acceptance over time. It takes a lot of time, and if you pretend to care at the start, it will be evident that you did not care if you stop showing up a few weeks down the road. If you want to be a friend, be a friend.

Check on this person every few weeks, every month for a while, and remember every calendar event. Birthdays, Mother's Day, Father's Day, Christmas, and even the anniversary of the child's death is a day of sadness and remembrance. Check in and be the smile. If tears flow, then sit, listen, and let them flow. If laughter is involved, laugh. Everyone grieves differently.

My friends Dawn, Laura, and Cheri were the friends who checked on me after Jacob died. I can't express how much this meant to me that they thought about me days, months, and years after Jacob's death. And they still do.

Dawn was able to be a friend while her own daughters were grieving Jacob's loss. Laura offered friendship with no strings attached. She listened without judgment or instruction.

Cheri had lost a brother when she was young and understood the endless grief that accompanies the unexpected loss of a young person. Cheri is a talker. You know the friend—chatty and funny and has something to say about everything. She's a hoot, and I love being around her hearty laughter.

But Cheri was quiet and all ears when she visited me. She listened and offered neither reasons nor solutions. She knew what to do. They all did. Presentness. Be there. Be quiet. Be a Dawn, Laura, or Cheri to your friends.

DO NOT SAY STUPID STUFF

E ver.
 This includes these little gems I heard at Jacob's funeral and the ones other parents have shared with me:

1. "God just needed Jacob in Heaven," or "It was God's Will." Oh, for goodness' sake, seriously?!? For what? You're telling me that God, Creator of the Universe, woke up on December 6th and yelled out, "Hey, I need Jacob up here stat! Go get him now, and I don't care how you do it."

No, sorry, the God I serve lost His Son on a cross. My God knows how horrible it is to lose a child. If I had a fraction of the power of God, I might have done more than a few hours of darkness and an earthquake the day my child was killed.

I thank my God that my son is with His Son today. But not because "God needed another angel" or because Jacob is "looking down on all of us" or "smiling down from Heaven." No offense for good intentions but saying that God took my child to work in Heaven on some project is horrifying to me and to other parents who have lost children.

I had to listen to the graphic forensic story of Jacob's death, over and over and over for almost a year in preparation for the trial. Do you really want to tell me that God planned that horrible event? Or do you just want to give me a hug? That's what I thought.

2. "Jacob's work on Earth is done." Shut the front door! What was he working on? Why did he finish so soon?

3. "Jacob is watching over us from Heaven." No, no, he's not. He's there, but he did not turn into an archangel. He's not a cherub or a ghost walking about, searching for his way.

4. "Bill sends his condolences." What the heck? Stop. If Bill is not there, the parents, spouse, and siblings don't really need to know that he is not there. Don't add a negative that someone was just too busy, too sick, or too anything else to make it to the funeral.

Later down the road, when the friends stop coming to visit, the family will remember all the weird stuff they were told about their child, brother, or spouse. Don't be the one they remember talking about why Bill couldn't make it. Or that this horrific event was "meant to be." Be the one who was there to just be there.

5. "You will get through this. You will get past this. You are stronger than you think. Time will heal. In time, you will forget." No, I won't, and it won't. I promise I won't. Unless I get a lobotomy, I will NEVER forget that my child died - five years, ten years, fifteen years, or twenty years. I remember it all quite well and always will.

There is no getting over, through, beyond, behind, or any other brilliant direction you might muster up from grief and loss of a loved one. We remember forever because that is what we are supposed to do. Most cultures and religions say to honor the dead—not forget about them.

Sue "Amma" Moore was a sweet and kind lady, James's grandmother, and the boys' great-grandma. We loved her so very much.

Her son Harry passed away at age 55, leaving her childless as his little brother, and Amma's second-born had passed away some 53 years prior, just after his birth. Lucky Jack.

When Amma was in her last days on this earth, she spoke through tears of the death of Lucky Jack. Her broken heart was just as broken years after Lucky Jack had died as it was when she'd first lost him. She was excited to be reunited soon with both her children, her husband, and her friends, and she asked us not to grieve for her as she was going to a happy place.

Think of Amma before you make any false promises about time. These promises are really just a way of saying the death is not important and the parent has no right to grieve the loss of a child more than a few months or years or for any set time.

It troubles me that many professionals and grief counselors believe there is a set time for grief—a particular path each person must endure to get to the other side of grief. It troubles me because it is a lie. A terrible lie.

Here is the awful truth. You will NEVER get over the death of someone you loved. Ever. Because you loved your child, spouse, parent, brother, or sister, your brain cannot forget. You cannot erase memories linked to this type of connection. This is not a broken heart—remember. It is a changed brain, a download to the operating system, if you will. Let me quickly reassure you that you will not and do not want to forget. Instead, let me show you how to find joy in remembering.

6. "Be grateful you have other children to care for." And they might throw in "What a blessing." This one makes me want to grab the person and shake hard until mixed. Gee whiz, can you insult a parent any more than that?

My two boys were grieving the loss of their best friend and brother. Jacob had another brother and one sister from his dad and stepmom—and last time I checked, they are all still grieving the loss of their brother as well.

Having other children is neither a blessing nor a burden as it relates to traumatic grief. I didn't need someone to remind me that I had two sweet innocent children who felt the same way I did.

This is a nightmare for a parent. I'm destroyed, and I must help my children because they are equally destroyed, and I don't know what to do for any of us. Rubbing this in a parent's or spouse's face is not a comfort. Someone might grab you and shake you like a Polaroid picture. I might, if I catch you doing it.

7. Not a bad answer but can be taken too far: "I am so sorry, I have no idea what it's like to lose a child. I don't know what I would do. No one should bury a child. I can't imagine what you're going through."

You're right, you don't, until you do. And you will, or you might. And you're not prepared. But neither was I.

Sadly, I'm not sure I can prepare you. I can only promise you that you will suffer because we all do. There is hope and healing. There will be happiness again. Your brain is wired to handle this event when it arises. Understanding the brain can help you understand how to deal with grief. And stop blaming it on your heart, God, or karma.

WHAT CAN I SAY AT THE FUNERAL?

So, what can you say at a funeral? More forgiving, but still lacking in full meaning, is the ever-popular "I'm sorry." There are no words in the English language that properly describe what is to be said to the parent after the loss of a child. This goes for spouses, siblings, children—anyone. There are no words.

We should wonder why there are no words in the English language for this event. In fact, we are meant to say very little. I have grown accustomed to "I'm sorry" and "I'm sorry for your loss" as standard practice for most people trying to show that they truly care. I will typically answer back, "I'm sorry, too," followed by an appreciative smile. Therefore, if you must say anything, "I'm sorry" is totally acceptable.

"I loved Jacob so much," "He was my best friend," "I don't know how life will be without him," or "My heart hurts for my friend." These are the heartfelt cries of close friends and family. These go without judgment and without suggestion. If you are suffering as a friend, girlfriend, best friend, cousin, grandparent, or schoolmate, you have every right to share this with the family. I still recommend keeping it brief at the funeral, but families want to know that their loved one touched another life in a positive way. This is good medicine.

A young man waited near the end of the line to see our family at Jacob's funeral. As someone would enter the line, he would step back to the end until he was truly the last person to chat with us. He was a big guy, but he was younger and much shyer than he looked at first. When he finally made it to talk with us, he was choked up.

"Hi, Ms. Moore, my name is Trey. You probably don't know who I am," he continued. "But, about six months ago, Jacob visited me. I was really sick from taking meth for months," Trey explained. "Jacob wanted to help me. He took me to church on Wednesday nights because I was afraid to go Sunday mornings. I just want you to know that, well, he changed my life. I've been off meth for a couple months, and I still plan to keep coming to church."

As Trey finished, we gathered him in our arms and cried. I thanked him for sharing this with us.

This was good medicine. Heart-wrenching. Beautiful. Good medicine. This young man Helped us Heal a tiny bit. Thousands of tears dropped on the church floor that evening. Most of them were the tears of brothers, sisters, parents, and grandparents who could not bear the loss of our little Jacob. But the tears of the many children who filled that church were heartbreaking.

This one child loved our son for giving him Hope that he could Heal from his addiction and see a brighter day. Stardust was falling all over that room.

Intermission over.

REALLY BAD ODDS

After Jacob's death, my husband James and I were not having any luck keeping the marriage together. The sudden traumatic death of a child can often destroy a marriage, and ours was no exception. We tried, but I was drowning in grief, and James was lost about what to say or do; the odds were against us. Counselors wanted to talk about our marriage, not our grief. Our marriage was not broken. We were. I was. The space in my heart that cared about James was replaced by a black hole of mourning. I withdrew into a world of my own where there was no room for him.

Although the marriage didn't make it, individually, we did, and the boys did. There were lots of mistakes, pain, and more tragedies to endure. But, somehow, with God and the people He placed in our paths, we all began to heal.

BURYING MORE FAMILY

I n the months and years that followed Jacob's death, my brother Bob would pass away in 2012 from a heart disorder. He was jogging down the road with his wife, Lori, when he simply dropped, and his heart stopped. My sister Janet would die from the many health issues she had suffered from accidents as a younger woman.

My mother became ill and lost her leg from the knee down. She passed away in December 2008 from a blood clot that traveled from her leg to her heart—the very same way we lost my brother Bo. My mother buried her firstborn in 2003, and I buried my firstborn in 2003. My mother was buried on the anniversary of Jacob's death.

My dad passed away in 2014 from pneumonia and a very bad heart. Dad had endured many heart surgeries over the years from 1984 until his death. Somehow Dad had managed to outlive both of his heart doctors.

But when I think of the losses in my family over the years and how I carried them along, I always remind myself that I did not carry them alone.

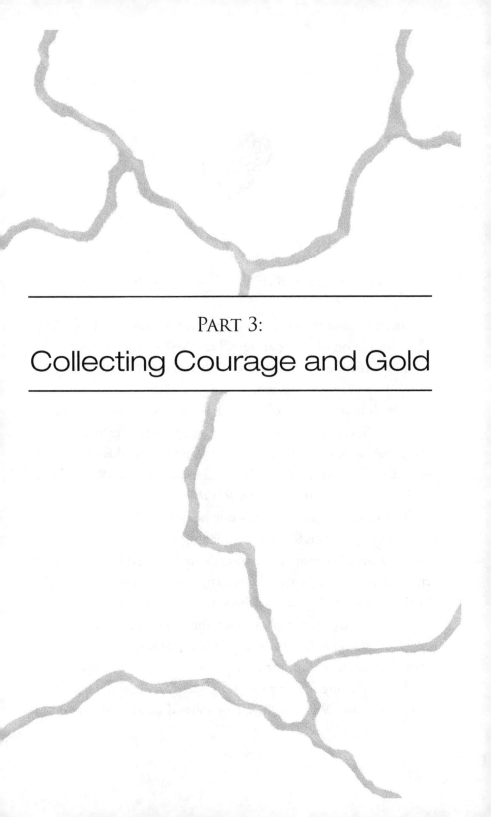

PART 3:
Collecting Courage and Gold

THE MEDICINE BAG AND THE PYRE

J ust four months after burying Jacob in his American Eagle
shirt, Corona T, and bare feet, I received a call from my brother
Bob. As I mentioned before, Bob was often the bearer of bad
news. This was no exception.

My dear friend John "Spotted Horse" Arrasmith had passed
suddenly. Spotted Horse had allowed me to help him work on several movie projects over the years, and he had worked on dozens,
including *The Last of the Mohicans*, *Teenage Mutant Ninja Turtles*,
Follow the River, and *Dances with Wolves*.

I recorded scripts for him while he was working on *Follow the
River*. My special crafty gift was making turkey feathers look like
eagle feathers. Spotted Horse was talented in everything else, from
creating authentic Native American deerskin apparel to crafting
intricate beadwork and headdresses. If you watched *Dances with
Wolves*, you saw the American flag, the beaver skin and bear claw
necklace, the arrows, and many other clothing items that were
owned or made by him for that movie.

I tagged along with him to Tennessee for a business trip to the
home of Hank Williams, Jr. Hank showed us around his and his

father's collection of vehicles and chatted about songs and song-writing. Hank gave me some names and phone numbers of folks who could help with my songwriting and publishing, and he signed his latest album for my mom. Hank is an amazing gentleman.

John Spotted Horse had been a true friend over the years, and my heart was broken that I would no longer have my friend in my life.

I traveled from Georgia to Kentucky and attended the funeral with my brother Bob. It was hard to say goodbye to another person that soon after Jacob had died. Around my neck, I wore the green leather medicine bag on a sinew string that Spotted Horse had made for me for prayer and healing, and the hand-carved deer bone feather on a beaded necklace he had given me for helping on a movie project.

I said goodbye, kissed him on the cheek, placed a note in the coffin, hugged his sweet family, and decided that John would have been happier if he had been set afire atop a pyre somewhere on his farm. This was how we had said goodbye to his beloved horse a few years before. But alas, there are laws against such things. Even in Kentucky. It's a real shame.

What was different about this funeral from any I had attended before my son's death? Even though I was sad and grieving, I didn't cry like I expected I would. Out of tears? Maybe. But John was a Christian, and somehow, I felt comfort knowing where he was. I had spent the last four months reminding myself that Jacob was not gone, just elsewhere, and now John was elsewhere as well. I had been healing in my grief. I knew death as normal and natural—sad and heartbreaking, but a normal and natural part of life.

I saw my friend John Spotted Horse in the coffin from the back of the room, but I could also picture Jacob lying there. It would be the case for many years and many family funerals to come. Every death, every funeral, was a reburial of my son along with the dearly departed. This was, unfortunately, very normal. And strangely a part of the acceptance of the loss.

The area where Jacob's coffin had sat at the front of my church was seared into my brain, like the barrel of burning Trixie Belden books years before. Each time I went to that church, I saw the shadow of his coffin. I would learn to see a cross there. But it was going to take time. Everyone's clock moves at a different speed when it comes to grief. And mine was on slo-mo.

PEARL JAM'S "BLACK"

A few months after Spotted Horse passed, my brother James and sister-in-law Sherry arrived at my house to visit. How do you mend a broken heart? Family Karaoke Night, of course. We traveled to a karaoke bar down the road and settled in for a night of singing. Music is good medicine, and anything good was better than what my family had been through.

While we sang, a small group of men walked in together. I didn't recognize any of them but found out they had traveled 12 hours from the mid-Ohio area for a traditional Southern Baptist wedding and were seeking out a little more excitement than punch and white wedding cake to finish their evening.

Adam was among the group, and he and my sister-in-law chatted. He asked about me. She told him my hurtful history. When Adam mustered the courage to say his first hello to me, he leaned over with his back against the wall beside me and said, "I won't hurt you."

My mouth opened in a "Wha?" But instead I said, "I know you won't." I laughed so hard. We both did. It was funny and sweet at the same time. The worst pickup line ever—but it would eventually work.

The subject changed quickly, and we asked him to get up there and sing something. He agreed but only if Pearl Jam's "Black" were available. Unfortunately for him and lucky for the rest of us, that song was available, and his small group of men stood up and sang. To this day, my ringtone for Adam is Pearl Jam's "Black."

I thought for many years that the song had no lyrical connection to me whatsoever, that it was just a happy memory of a small turning point in my life. But years later I read the lyrics and a comment that co-writer Eddie Vedder made in the *Pearl Jam Twenty* book. "It's about first relationships. The song is about letting go," Vedder explained. "It's very rare for a relationship to withstand the Earth's gravitational pull and where it's going to take people and how they're going to grow. I've heard it said that you can't really have a true love unless it was a love unrequited. It's a harsh one, because then your truest one is the one you can't have forever."

It seemed there was a message in there for me and for Adam. We had loved and lost. The paths were different, but the outcome of sadness and grief were the same. All the bad relationships had turned our worlds to black.

The karaoke ended. Adam and his group traveled 12 hours back to Ohio, but Adam and I stayed in touch. We would chat by phone, sharing stories and pain from past relationships, discussing the cheaters and the liars in our lives, and encouraging each other to recover and be happy.

We talked about loss and Jacob. We also talked about dreams for the future. How life may have some hope left for him and for me. We realized we had a lot in common: writing, drawing, Boy Scouts, movies, and music. We both wanted to finish college. And we realized it was a comfort to talk to each other. And for the first time, talking to someone about Jacob was effortless and comforting.

One evening, while we chatted, I watched what must have been the space shuttle flying fast over my little home in Georgia. Within a few minutes, or maybe just seconds, Adam watched the shuttle fly over his little house in Ohio. It was a falling-star kind of moment that we will never forget.

Although the distance seemed to evaporate at that moment, the reality of the distance meant there was no serious discussion of whether the relationship was to go any further than friendship. My life was certainly too complicated to add anyone to the lineup. Adam had a great job and plans to travel. I had a business to run and two boys to raise. We resolved to be friends.

FIGHT CLUB

Mid-Summer 2004, I was driving home alone and realized there was a car following me, but I thought nothing more of it. Probably a neighbor, I thought.

I shot up my driveway and right into the garage in my little convertible Volkswagen Bug. When I opened my car door, a man stepped into the space between me and the door, scaring the life out of me. "Can you give me directions to Sandy Run?" the man asked.

At this point, I knew. I just knew I was going to die. I needed to think. I needed to run. I shakily replied, "You mean Lake Joy Road?" I picked a road far from Sandy Run to assure myself that I was, indeed, about to die. "Yes, that's it," he answered unconvincingly. "Okay," I said, my voice still shaking with fear. "Let me get out, and I have a map in my purse."

He stepped back. I stepped out of the car, closed the door and then bolted. But he was ready, and his arm was around my neck before I could escape, and his other hand was holding my hair as he pulled me in the direction of his wide-open car door in the driveway.

As I fought back, he struggled to put me into his vehicle. I dropped my weight to the ground beside his driver's side door. We wrestled around, punching, scratching, and pulling until I was thrown behind his vehicle.

There it was. His license plate. AKV0**3. I started yelling the number at him, and he jumped in his vehicle, door open, staring at me. I ran, leaped over my purse that lay in the middle of the driveway, and grabbed Isaac's wooden Louisville Slugger from the corner of the garage. I started swinging, yelling the license plate even louder. "**AKV0**3! AKV0**3!**"

My hair was mangled and some of it was missing, my clothes were disheveled, and makeup, blood, and tears were in all the wrong places on my face. I may have scared the heck out of him as he closed his car door and floored it in reverse, taking out purple and pink azaleas all the way down my driveway to the road.

My dad was a trained batting coach, so when I was growing up, he became my batting coach and taught me how to hit a baseball. My five brothers were good at baseball, but I was a bona fide tomboy and although I couldn't catch a ball very well, I was a fantastic hitter. Hitting took true technique, and I found it easy to simply decide where to send the ball with the bat. I favored the wood sluggers.

I taught my sons to bat, and Isaac had true talent. He favored the wood sluggers as well and, as luck would have it, he kept one handy. During my life, I have chased off a fox, a coyote, and now, a would-be serial killer. Each time with a wooden baseball bat in hand. I thank my dad for the lessons, Isaac for his love of the game, and God for putting the Louisville Slugger there to save me.

I ran into the house, screaming the plate number over and over. "AKV0**A3"! I hit the wooden bat on the table to get someone to help me before I forgot the number. I was missing a shoe.

Then I saw the pen. I grabbed it from the table and wrote the number on the front of Isaac's white plastic school binder " A K V

0 * * 3" and then collapsed in a chair. By this time, everyone was in the kitchen. I briefly told the story, and Isaac ran out the door and down the street trying to catch the attacker, to no avail.

I was searching for my phone to call 911 when I heard someone yelling from the phone. It had been pushed around my belt to my back during the fight. And when I'd landed on the concrete, I'd butt-dialed Adam. "Sylvia, Sylvia!" Adam was yelling. He had heard the screaming and then me yelling the license plate over and over.

He was 12 hours away, with no way to help; he was torn between hanging up to call 911 and staying on the line so he would know my outcome. Can you imagine his horror as he listened to what was happening?

911 was called. And using the plate number, the police quickly found the young man (let's call him Rusty) at home in his bed. His car engine was still running. The car door was wide open in his driveway. My hair, along with the purple and pink azalea blossoms, lay in the front seat.

Rusty had attempted to kidnap two 12-year-old girls just weeks before behind the local grocery store, and he tried to capture a jogger in a neighborhood a couple miles from mine. All of us picked him from the lineup.

The other three girls also recognized his vehicle. But I had seen the plate number. "You stopped a would-be serial killer," the DA remarked. "I just wanted to live," I replied.

No one could explain why Rusty was in MY driveway that night. "I just wanted to kill someone, like Tim," the attacker told police that night. Tim (name also changed) was the man who had murdered my son only eight months before. This explanation was mind-blowing to the DA and the detectives. Tim and Rusty had been friends for years.

Now riddle this, Batman: Rusty wanted to kill someone. The other three victims were unrelated and unknown to me and Rusty, and Tim for that matter. The police fully believe that there were most likely other women that did not come forward. But Rusty claimed he had no idea I was Jacob's mother, but he followed me across town and all the way up my driveway. The coincidence was driving the prosecution and the defense crazy. It was not sitting well with me nor my family either.

Because I did not die, and because Georgia does not have an attempted murder charge, Rusty was charged with kidnapping and assault and battery.

Do I believe God puts people in places where they should be on occasion? Sure, read your Bible. But was *I* supposed to stop him? Why couldn't I stop Tim from killing Jacob? Why didn't God spare me another horrific event? I simply don't know. I was a very poor choice for a fistfight with a grown man.

There is no explanation. But no one died. It was meant to end there. But maybe I was the one who needed to stop him. Or maybe—just maybe—he was supposed to stop me. Maybe we were meant to stop each other.

Up to that point, I was so sad at the loss of Jacob, I was in danger of being careless with my own life. I was finding it difficult to care for anyone in my life. It was hard to talk with the boys about their brother or how they hurt. I had no answers for them, and I was struggling to recover and be a good mom.

My marriage to James had ended, and I didn't feel anything for him as I had before. To put it bluntly, I was grieving so deeply that I didn't care about anything or anyone, including myself. I didn't care if I lived or died. And I made sure God knew that every chance I could.

YOU DON'T TALK ABOUT IT

"You don't talk about Fight Club" is the famous line from the movie *Fight Club*. I rarely tell this story of being pulled across my driveway, facing the inside of a stranger's car and what seemed certain death.

I mean, how do you start that conversation with a friend? "Well, Marge, the funniest thing happened on the way home from the store the other day …" Nope, too weird. I had just lost a son. What trumps that? I mean, I had the Ace of Pain already in my hand, my son's murder, and the trial was in a month! Any other card had no serious face value in comparison.

But I was in a fight that night. And the movie had rules: "If this is your first night at Fight Club, you have to fight." And I fought! I fought with everything I had. I was ready to fight as long as it took to be free. I fought for my life. I wanted to live. I really needed to live. And that moment changed me forever.

Yes, I wanted and needed to live. I needed to be there for my boys. Oh, my Lord, if I had died, what would have become of those two young men? Dang it, I wanted my life back.

The very next month, I was in the courtroom as Tim was sentenced to life in prison for the murder of my son. "I didn't know Jacob," he admitted in court. But we did. And it hurt my heart that he had killed my son for no apparent reason.

The jury was also told that meth had made Tim see my son as a monster, instead of the sweet, giving, green-eyed guy he was. But meth was not on trial, Tim was. Tim ended the trial with a confession, then he headed to prison, and the rest of us went home to begin a long journey back to normal.

I was sad for Tim's family. Two sons were lost when Jacob was killed. We lost Jacob to eternity, and Tim's family lost him to the Georgia Department of Corrections for life. Tim had been in trouble as a child; his siblings were known well in the juvenile court system. Tim was only 17 when he shot Jacob; he spent his 18th birthday in prison, awaiting trial.

About a month after Jacob died, Tim was brought into court for a hearing. He had evidently been in a fight with his face. The DA told us Tim had had an argument with a "rather big fellow" in the jail courtyard regarding possession of a basketball. The big fellow had won the argument. Tim's face had lost.

Tim's mom was also arrested and convicted for hiding Tim in a drug house in the woods a few counties away and possibly tampering with the weapon. While I still felt sadness for Tim, I found myself disappointed and angry with his mother for quite some time. The police captured Tim by circling the drug house with helicopters and brought in canine units on the ground. His mom was arrested with less pomp and circumstance.

I would sit in that same courtroom a few months down the road for Rusty's trial, and surprisingly, I felt sad for Rusty as well. Sad that his family was losing him. Sad that he seemed so sad and scared and lost. Sad that he had dropped out of school, and no one had seemed to notice. Sad for his mom. Sad that he was so young and strung out on drugs. Rusty needed love. I was sad that no one had stepped in to help him before he'd gone too far.

This was another reason I needed to live: to do everything I could to keep my sons from heading down the path Tim and Rusty took. To keep their eyes looking upward and forward. To teach them to live and love and forgive. I had a way to go first. But it was just around the bend, and I could hear Pearl Jam's "Black" playing in the distance.

PTSD

You do not understand PTSD until you have PTSD. It is bizarre. One moment you are walking through the open mall, then you turn a corner and start down a small hallway to the bathroom. Just ahead, a man is walking toward you (most likely coming out of the bathroom), and you are frozen. The space around you gets small and dark, and you are looking through a tunnel. Fear hits like a brick in your face, and you go into an internal fight stance. Fight or flight. The next time someone suggests going to the mall, you decline.

From what my doctor told me, the trauma from Jacob's death made it statistically probable that I would suffer from PTSD. Then add to the trauma intrusive memories, recurring dreams about Jacob falling from a balcony, flashbacks of his body on the gurney, and emotional overload.

But when Rusty decided to spar with me in my driveway, in the hopes of taking me back to his house, he heaped the fear of physical harm upon the fear of losing another child, with a side dish of "I'm freaking scared of my own shadow." I had trouble thinking, sleeping, remembering, and eating. I felt cut off from the world and avoided people and conversation as much as possible.

But several things occurred concurrently that pushed me away from the brink of despair and gloom.

First, the two trials. I had closure on both the murderer and the would-be lady killer. In both courtrooms, I found myself forgiving the murderer and the attacker. I did not run to the judge and say, "Free this man, Your Honor … I forgive him." But there was the release of any hate.

I did not hate either man. Not my son's killer or my attacker. I told Rusty in court that he had our prayers and forgiveness, and I hoped that he would find peace someday. I couldn't say anything to Tim in court, but I did walk away knowing I harbored no animosity toward him. I knew that to be healed, I had to first forgive.

The second key to my successful fight to heal from trauma and PTSD was Adam. Our friendship grew over the months leading up to the trials. In 2005, Adam transferred from the post office in Ohio to the one in Middle Georgia and purchased a home.

He had made up his mind: if we were going to have a chance at more than friendship, he would need to meet me halfway. He drove 12 hours with all his belongings and a screaming male cat to live nearer to me, and I moved my heart a thousand miles closer to his heart. It was a good trade.

SCRUPLES IS GOOD MEDICINE

I was a big basket of mess—and yet Adam was there for me. He was working out some of his own life events, and we were great company for each other. I don't think "misery loves company." I believe great company fixes great misery.

Young lovers buy the broken-heart necklaces. You know, half worn by him, and half worn by her. When together, the halves make one perfect heart. Well, that was Adam and me. But we were two separate broken hearts that found each other. We didn't fit together perfectly at first, but we worked on it until we did.

Adam had been raised by his hard-working single mother of three. His father lived in the same town but had abandoned the family when Adam was very small to enjoy a life of drug use and crime. At about 13 or 14, Adam realized that if he did not leave the neighborhood where his family lived, he would end up on a very bad path.

Gangs and drugs were prevalent in his neighborhood, and the school wasn't any better. Adam saw no way out unless he physically left his home. His mom and he agreed that he could live with another family during the school semesters so he would have a better chance of success. And he did. His foster dad, Erol, instilled discipline, Godliness, and kindness, and gave Adam a proper father figure to whom he could aspire.

After graduation, Adam and his buddy Donovan joined the Army and headed from Ohio to Columbus, Georgia, to train for the Army Airborne Infantry. Adam was injured during training and spent a year at the military base building back his health before heading home to Ohio, where he worked his way up quickly in the postal service to mail carrier.

After Adam caught his girlfriend cheating, he resolved to be single. The Army injury and the long recovery followed by heart-ache had left him depressed. He decided he would focus on getting a degree and possibly traveling. And then, as fate would have it, he went to this boring Southern Baptist Georgia wedding.

As the trials of Tim and Rusty passed, Adam, the boys, and I got to know each other. I discovered Adam was younger than me. He discovered he really liked kids. Well, at least my two kids.

In fact, my sons came to love Adam very quickly—as did I. Adam is a true friend to his friends and a true lover of those he loves. "Scruples" he calls it. "Scruples" is good medicine. And scruples, along with Erol's formula of discipline, Godliness, and kindness, was just what the boys needed as they continued to mourn the loss of their brother and best friend.

HAVE COURAGE, YOU HURT
BECAUSE YOU LOVE

Parents go through indescribable emotional trauma with the loss of a child. Regardless of the age of the child or the parent, this loss is deep and painful and causes permanent damage. Lovers, brothers, husbands, and wives are no exception to this deep loss. To pretend like someone will bounce back from this event is denying the truth about Love in the first place. We Love or we Love Not. When we Love, we are connected in body and soul to the person we love.

When we are separated from the person we love, we are, at the very least, sad. Jesus walked the earth knowing He was going to die, be resurrected, and then live forever. He knew His friends would join him. Jesus told his friends, "²In My Father's house are many [a]mansions; if *it were* not *so,* [b]I would have told you. I go to prepare a place for you. ³And if I go and prepare a place for you, I will come again and receive you to Myself; that where I am, *there* you may be also." (John 14:2,3 NKJV). This also meant Lazarus.

Jesus loved his friend Lazarus and knew where Lazarus was going when he died, and yet "³⁵Jesus wept" when Lazarus died.

Jesus was sad. He missed His friend, and He was sad for Mary and Martha, who had lost their brother. John 11:35 NKJV proves that even the Son of God felt emotion and loss. It is normal and natural to be sad.

It takes courage to begin to heal from loss. So, start with Love. It was Love that caused us to hurt from the loss. To start healing, you must practice love again. For me, I was broken in many pieces—an emotional train wreck after Jacob's death, but I loved Daniel and Isaac. Every time I showed I loved them or thought about my love for them, I healed a bit. Bit by bit, memories took the place of nightmares, and laughter returned to our home.

PART 4:

7 to Heal

HELP!!!

The place to start is to get HELP. Help yourself. Get help from others. Get professional help with serious depression and thoughts of death, dying, or even suicide.

Most losses cause grief. But when grief lingers or just freaking hurts, then getting help with grief is the right path. Grief recovery or grief support groups are a wonderful place to start. Discussing the loss or trauma and exploring why you are stuck in grief can be the first step to true healing.

You can start having the courage to help yourself by understanding your grief is not controlled by a set timeline. And you are not sharing your grief with anyone. Accept that your grief and pain are your grief and pain. Not your friend's or your mother-in-law's, not even your spouse's or your child's. It is yours. Do not let anyone railroad it away from you. Once you claim it, you can begin to heal.

If you are wondering, "Oh my gosh, do I have to carry around all this pain forever?", the answer is "No." Have Courage! Grief is just a chapter in your story. A small book in the library of you! You need to admit it is part of your story. You need to learn how to read it, own it, and find a nice place for it on the shelf. Stop wearing it on your forehead like a badge.

Feel the pain, feel the sadness, feel the loneliness. These are the emotions that go hand in hand with loss, grief, and trauma, and you must carry your grief inside all these emotions. You can't hide from it. You certainly should not deny it. And you cannot pretend you are okay. It is okay to feel the way you feel.

As crazy as it sounds, you may feel like you are losing your mind. Perhaps you can't remember an appointment or a name or a simple recipe. These are normal reactions to great pain and distress. The greater your love for the one you lost, the greater the emotions. Remember: no one knows exactly how you feel.

With that said, sometimes grief, trauma, or heartbreak can lead down the dark road to serious depression.

Help from Doctors

If you feel that your grief may be spiraling down that dark path of hate and self-destruction, get medical help. It is normal to have sleeping issues, sadness, over- or under-eating, and trouble concentrating. But when symptoms become so heavy they feel like a weight on your chest, and added to the mix are extreme anger, apathy, health issues, lack of self-care, or hopelessness, then it is time to talk with your family and a doctor.

Talking with a doctor is not an admission that you somehow failed grief. Every person I have interviewed, including myself, has had feelings of despair. When you are ready to talk about healing from grief, then do it. Don't wait. There is no magic timeline for grief recovery. I waited years to ask for help. I regret not seeking the solution sooner. Grief is one of those things my family taught me to keep inside. So I did.

Isaac was suffering in high school after he had lost his brother and best friend. He either slept too much or not at all. He was active in baseball as an extracurricular activity, but he was spiraling into depression, overcome with grief and afraid to tell anyone about it. When he finally reached out to a friend about his despair, he was immediately pushed into a conversation with a doctor. That was an eye-opener for Isaac. He knew he needed to start helping himself get better. He had to deal with the emotions and start living in the grief, not hiding from it.

Help—You Can't Run Until You Walk

In June 2014, Adam proposed to me on bended knee. I had certainly feared marriage—or failing at it again—but our relationship had already outlived any other relationship from the past. In all honesty, we had been together so many years and by that point, we considered ourselves an old married couple. But the kids and the pastor disagreed, so a wedding was planned.

Just days before the wedding, I fell on my butt while skating with the family at the local rink. At first, I had no idea my hip was injured. The wedding went on with nothing more than a big bruise on my bottom. I kept up my usual running schedule of about six-plus miles a week. But within a couple of years, I was suddenly unable to run without pain. When the pain began to wake me in the night, I saw a doctor and received the bad news that I needed a new hip. The MRI showed an out-of-whack hip joint with almost zero protective cartilage. This meant sawing off the leg just below the hip and installing my new titanium leg and hip. I would have a big freaking scar down the front of my leg and I would set off metal detectors for the rest of my life, but I was more concerned because I wanted to run again. I ate so I could run and I ran so I could eat. I had already started to gain weight and the muscles in my legs had begun to atrophy before the surgery.

The surgery went very well, and I named my new metal hip-and-leg combo Ivar, after Ivar the Boneless, the crippled Viking who, according to legend, conquered his enemies without bones in his legs. I was diagnosed with osteoporosis and arthritis. And it seemed ole Ivar suffered from *osteogenesis imperfecta* (weak bones). Despite Ivar's disabilities, he was wise and cunning, and a skilled and strategic leader.

"I want to run again," I informed Dr. Dustin Hoffman (yes, that is his real name). The doctor understood but said he could not promise that I would "run" again. Most patients were content with riding a bike a year after surgery, I was told. "I still want to run," I insisted.

"If you want to run again," my doctor instructed, "you must first learn to walk again."

Before the surgery, I walked with a terrible limp. My injured leg was shorter. Along with the pain each step invited, I was quite a sight to see hobbling from Point A to Point B each day.

After the surgery, I was instructed to use a walker. Yep, an old-lady walker with the fancy tennis balls on the bottom and everything. After several days with the walker, I graduated to new crutches. I preferred the crutches because I could move faster around the house with fewer restraints. Stairs were frightening, so I mastered the first floor. By the end of the first week, I had moved on to a walking cane I called my Walking Dead. My brother Jeff made it for me from a baseball bat covered in barbed wire. (Try getting that through TSA). I then graduated to my Bo staff, (fighting stick). I conceded to my family's wishes and placed a tennis ball on the end, but it was the perfect walking stick. Besides, I could take out bad guys if any crossed my path of recovery.

When I visited the doctor for my first post-surgery checkup, he insisted that I start walking without assistance as soon as possible. "If you don't start walking, you will never heal," he instructed.

"I want to run soon," I announced.

"There can be no running again until you master walking again," he rallied back over his chart.

When I inquired about pain meds, he said, "You don't need pain medication. You need to walk." When I suggested physical therapy, he said, "No, only walking, just walking."

So, I started walking. I walked everywhere. I mastered the stairs and the gravel driveway. By the next visit to Dr. Hoffman, I was wearing some low-heel pumps and a cute dress.

"You don't look like a patient who just had hip surgery," my doctor bragged.

"No sir, I want to run again," I announced.

One day I was standing out front when a fox grabbed one of my chickens. Without thinking about it, I started running toward the fox, who unhappily dropped his lunch. With my chick safely in her pen, I assessed any damage from the run. None. "No power in the 'verse can stop me," I thought. (That's from *Firefly*, 2003.)

In less than a year after my surgery, I was jogging around Serenity Farm and Firefly Pond. I still walk as much as possible, but I am so happy that I can run at all. It's not the same as competing in a 5K or 10K run. My metal hip doesn't like the mistreatment of that kind of hard running. I carry Ivar with every stride. But I can run because I first walked.

Learning to live again after the death of a loved one is similar to learning to walk again. You have to have the courage to help yourself in the process. You will have a big freaking scar down the middle of your heart. You will never be exactly the same as you were before the loss, divorce, or death, but you will live again. You will walk, and you will run again.

Helping yourself means taking baby steps at the beginning and teaching yourself how to heal. And you may need more time or less time with each step. Regardless of anything else you have read, there is no "schedule to recovery" for grief. You are taking your grief, along with the broken pieces of your heart and soul, with you. And you will be fine.

Help Your Family

Unfortunately, I didn't get time to help myself heal before I was facing two young men who were drowning in grief. Daniel was seven and Isaac sixteen when Jacob died. There were dozens of people at our home every day for a week. The DA and detectives visited daily as the manhunt for Jacob's murderer continued. There were a thousand friends and family members at the funeral. It was chaos.

Finally, when the crowds were gone, we focused on the boys and tried to ease the pain of the loss of their brother, with Christmas only a couple weeks away.

If you have children, they will need you when they suffer a great loss. Sometimes the process of helping your family leads to helping yourself recover as well. But remember that the same rules apply in grief recovery as in flying. When the oxygen masks drop down, put your own mask on before trying to help others with theirs. My flawed attempts to help my children after Jacob died were due to my unresolved grief. When I got help for the grief, I discovered all the other losses, grief, and traumas I had been carrying around that needed to be resolved as well. I began to fill my scars with Gold, and it was a eureka moment for me. I immediately knew how to throw the lifeline out to my boys.

There is a problem I see with some families, and it is exacerbated by social media: the pattern of encouraging raunchy behavior and the sharing of "dirty laundry." If there is not enough controversy going on in the family, someone will drum it up. There is always someone posting about a family problem or fight. If too many months go by without controversy, someone will create some and start the cycle all over again. Then, when real trauma, loss, or grief hits, like death or cancer, the already-splintered family implodes.

Help your family for generations to come. Be the head of the family that starts different traditions. Have a hard-working family, with bonding family traditions and philanthropy. Be anything but the next guest on *The Jerry Springer Show*. I have met Jerry Springer twice at political affairs in Cincinnati with my mom—he was a nice guy. But I never, ever wanted to be on his show. Neither should you.

Helping Your Grown Children with Grief

Losing his brother Jacob took a real toll on Isaac. Physically and mentally. From serious depression to anger issues. He was barely passing school, and I didn't recognize the depth of his depression. He hid it well with friendships, girlfriends, baseball, and other school activities. His teachers were helping him by being lax. And Isaac was using this as a crutch.

Once an honors student with a college degree in his near future, Isaac started to struggle to get even the simplest of tasks completed. It was no wonder that he nearly failed out in the first year of college. There were going to be tough decisions to make about his future. Decisions that were frightening to me.

We discussed his depression with his dad, and it was agreed by all three dads and both moms that Isaac should spend some time away from Middle Georgia—away from the influence of college-age friends. Far away. We sent him to Northern Kentucky to be with his dad and near our families while he went to college. We visited back and forth, and Isaac started making real progress. He seemed happier and had focus again. We discovered part of his focus was a young lady named Jessica.

Jessica and Isaac married in 2012 and returned to live in Middle Georgia. They had our first grandbaby, Ellowyn, in the summer of 2014.

Isaac didn't leave Jacob's memory behind in order to recover; he took the memory with him and learned to be happy again. Death of a brother is not a disease from which he could recover. It was not a scar that would fade. It was a life experience he had to learn to live with. And he made it as Gold as a Scar could get. He volunteered at church, helped with the youth there, and took youth-pastor classes at the Cincinnati Christian College I had once attended.

Isaac carried his memories, pain, and Gold Scars, and he shared these with others. In the process, he created a way through the darkness of loss to the light of helping others.

Isaac finished his studies and now enjoys a career as a senior software engineer. His little family of four also includes our only grandson, Elon Jacob.

As he explained it to me, 19 years later at age 35, Isaac still has occasional anxiety over the loss of his brother. He most likely always will. He misses his brother and thinks about him often. His memory is tied to the devastating, horrific death of his brother, and the memory will never completely fade. But he has courage and faith. And Gold Scars.

Recently, Elon was in an accident and cut his head. We all rushed to the hospital, making our way to the area where little

Elon lay, head bleeding, his injury looking much worse than it was. The event was frightening for Isaac and Jessica. Isaac became anxious when he saw the inside of the hospital emergency area. It brought back some bad memories. The fear of losing a child is normal for all parents, but for a parent who has suffered a great loss, the fear will bring the memory back to the surface to hang out for a while.

This is normal. Normal for Isaac, Jessica, Daniel, me, and the rest of our family. And this is normal for you. Living with our grief teaches us how to handle fear and loss. We don't forget. We just carry it better once we are healed.

Helping Your Young Child with Grief

While Isaac was away, Daniel was suddenly alone. He had James, Adam, and me, as well as Grandma Judy, but he had gone from being the youngest of three boys to being an only child for nearly two years. He begged to move to Kentucky or bring Isaac back. We increased our visits back and forth until Isaac moved home to Georgia with Jessica.

We didn't see it at first, but as Daniel got closer to his teens and then into high school, he began to withdraw. He was already a shy child, but his circle of friends became very small, just the guys in honors classes, and he lacked the courage for simple things like asking a girl to the prom or attending many functions that his friends enjoyed. He was grieving. The process had been delayed. But he was going through the same emotional rollercoaster his brother and I had experienced, just ten years later.

Daniel had the same trouble with college that Isaac had experienced. A really smart honors kid who is sad and depressed is a terrible student. He was just a little broken, and college needed to wait a bit. Daniel found his way through the depression and is a happy, healthy, and very handsome young man.

Delayed grief is common with young children. As a parent, grandparent, or caregiver of children, you can be there during the process to love and lend guidance and support through the troubling times. Allow the child to talk about the love and the loss. Encourage good memories. Be there to explain that there may not be many memories if the loss took place when the child was young. But their sibling, parent, or grandparent loved them very much. Share photos, stories, and letters if appropriate. Let the child catch up in their grief by remembering and healing.

Pay It Forward and Help Others When You Can

There will be others who will be in pain. And with Jacob's death, there were hundreds of close friends and family members who were hurting. Show some kindness to these folks in allowing them to speak to you about their loss. Don't have a "family only" funeral. Open the doors, open the coffin, and open your heart.

When the four parents were shopping for a coffin, the experience made me realize that this was real. Jacob was gone. But for everyone else, the shock of Jacob's death came when they saw his body in the coffin at the front of our church. One way we helped was to have the service at the church rather than a small funeral parlor. Everyone could come, everyone could share. We opened the casket and let his friends say goodbye. We stood in the church foyer and allowed anyone and everyone to come chat with us about Jacob. Everyone wanted or needed to say something, and we let it happen.

Helping means comforting others when you are still destroyed inside. Jenny was Jacob's girlfriend. Her loss and distress were equal to ours. She was devastated. Opening our home and heart to her was the first step. Giving her access to some of Jacob's personal items was a comfort to her. Our biggest challenge was finding her Christmas present from Jacob.

Jacob had put money down on a necklace a few weeks before he died. He had no receipt in his belongings, but we knew he had the necklace on layaway somewhere. So the phone calls and visits began. We traveled to every mall and jewelry store we could find, telling them about our son and his gift until we found the necklace. We paid the balance and gifted the necklace to Jenny before Christmas.

This small gift was our family's way of helping another person who was suffering from the loss of our son. You can find great joy in helping others heal, even when you are deep in your grief. Paying it forward helps heal you and those who loved your child, spouse, or parent.

Help Save and Protect Your Job, Career, Business

Don't forsake your work or career. Reach out to clients and customers and let them know you are healing. Pretending like nothing happened to save a deal is just wrong. No one believes you anyway, so just be honest.

Helping to save your business from the loss is important. I lost all interest in my career for several years after Jacob died. When I started the H-process and started seeing recovery on the horizon, I also wanted my career back. Sadly some clients had moved on. Others were faithful through the entire process. But it was still a rough road recreating my business after several years of disinterest.

Reach out to peers and get assistance. Hang on to the clients by keeping them posted on your experiences. Create a blog about healing, hope, and your recovery story. They will wait. Your courage and your desire to share with others will build on those relationships and form new ones.

Because grief and loss can rewire the brain a bit, get help from a peer to keep emails and information flowing in a timely fashion. Get help from your staff, family, friends, coworkers, or peers to ensure your calendar events are not missed or are rescheduled if necessary.

Do not let your competitors or coworkers see grief as your weakness. Yes, you are torn apart. But no, you are not weak. You are courageous and you are blood and bone, brain and heart, and right now, even if life is bad, this is your Life, and this is also your business, job, or career.

HEALING

Filling Wounds with Gold Scars

Healing from the death of a loved one is a lifelong journey. You loved; therefore, you still love. You will always love. Alfred, Lord Tennyson, wrote: "Tis better to have loved and lost than never to have loved at all." And nothing hurts as badly as the loss of a loved one. So what can you do to ease the pain and heal the broken heart?

First, there are going to be scars. When I realized that I did not FEEL healed from Jacob's death, it hit me: I had been looking for an eraser, and I should have been searching for a highlighter! I didn't need a way to FORGET what happened to my son. I needed a better way to remember.

I didn't set Jacob aside, forget about him, or suppress my grief or sadness. I took him with me along the recovery journey. I healed and continued to recover by facing his death, resolving the "I wish I coulda, woulda, shoulda" issues around his untimely death, and acknowledging my grief, guilt, pain, and losses were deep and needed courage, time, and attention to heal. It filled my wounds with Gold Scars. A much better way to remember.

When I turned away from my cancer diagnosis in 1987 and made the decision to ignore it as best I could until Isaac was born, I changed my brain a bit—a "reprogramming," you might say. I decided to do those things I always wanted to do. The things I should have done, but life had stepped in my way. I volunteered at church—setting out six months pregnant to be a counselor at a kids church camp.

I got down on my knees and prayed for healing my cancer, and I allowed others to pray for me. Was this the path perhaps I was meant to take, but I got lost? By retaking the path, was I healed? I'm not sure. Some would say yes. But I was, after all, healed. And I thanked God for my boys and for giving me a chance to be a mother of four. And I believe God had His hand in healing. This healing was not without scars.

Likewise, when Adam announced that he was enrolling in college in the Spring of 2007 and continuing until completion, I was so excited for him. He immediately suggested I do the same. "No way," I said. "I'm too old. I'll be 50 before I graduate." I had a lot of excuses.

"So?" Adam was not impressed.

"So, maybe I will," I corrected myself. And enroll I did.

A seven-year journey of the two of us juggling education, working, raising two grieving children, and keeping our bank accounts above zero ended in 2014, with me achieving the President's Scholar Award, being the Valedictorian of my university graduating class, and being honored as a student of "Greatness" with degrees in business, management, and IT.

I was 52 when I graduated. Adam graduated beside me, Summa Cum Laude and President's list with multiple degrees in psychology, public service, and IT. Daniel graduated from high school the following week with all honors. Isaac and Jessica gave birth to our first grandbaby, Ellowyn, the same summer. Adam and I got hitched in September 2014, and our wedding was featured on the BBC. It was a busy summer.

When I spoke to my graduating class, my speech, appropriately titled "Life Gets in the Way," shared how I'd moved through the traumatic events in my path to achieve a goal I had planned over 35 years earlier. And on a much deeper level, I shared how I not only lived out my dream, but I picked up Jacob's dream of a degree in business management as well and achieved it with honors, in his honor, in my honor, at the same college he had been attending when he'd died.

My family talks about Jacob often. We see his pictures and belongings every day.

Chat with friends and family about the happy or even funny events when your spouse, sibling, or child was alive. Put these memories in your pocket and bring them out when there's a rainy day. Every year on Mother's Day, Jacob's birthday, and the anniversary of Jacob's death, I pull out the stardust of memories and sprinkle it around the room. I remember, and I cry a little and smile a lot, or vice versa. There is a time to cry and remember, so find your time and put it on your schedule. Remembering life is healthy.

After a divorce, abuse, or other trauma, it is difficult to find a way to heal and forget the pain. The person that hurt you will only be a memory away. But you can say goodbye properly and heal from grief by attending a grief-recovery class.

Here's my website: www.SylviaMooreMyers.com. I have a link there where you can recover from grief, loss, trauma, divorce, abuse, and even the loss of a pet; I can also help with children who suffer from loss, grief, and trauma.

During your recovery, be careful to neither enshrine nor condemn the deceased, the cheating spouse, or the abuser. Making excuses for why someone hurt you is not a way to heal. Keeping the bedroom of a child untouched for many years is not healthy for you or your family.

Don't believe the lies your brain or society tells you: *I'm a bad mom. I'm a terrible friend. I did something that made my husband hurt me. It was my fault my boss sexually harassed me. I can't do this. I'm a failure.* No, you are not a failure. And if you believe you are, you will not recover from grief and loss. You will get stuck in the grief holding pattern and do nothing. Babe Ruth said, "Never let the fear of striking out get in your way." Well, no one walks up to bat and hits the ball by mistake either. So, get your bat, and let's go hit a few balls, shall we?

Crossing the Trident

Suppressing grief is not the way to heal. Wounds turn into scars, and scars just go with you everywhere you go.

I carried Jacob's memory like a proud battle scar and crossed over the Trident with all four of my babies, my broken heart, my lost relationships, permanent injuries from my attacker, my PTSD, and all my sins. I carried them up the hillside, crossed over the embankment and slid to the finish line with everything in tow.

Anyone who tells you there are stages of grief you must adhere to in order to be healed is wrong. There are no steps or stages. I mean there is NO Point A to Point E. No forgetting, getting over, getting past, or moving on. We carry our burdens, joys, memories, loves, and even enemies with us on our journey through life. Admitting this is okay. It is the beginning of healing and the beginning of being happy again.

Scars are part of the journey. Grief is as normal as rain in the Spring. It exists in the season in which it resides. Likewise, grief can be as harmful as a tornado and as unsettling as an earthquake. But there is a time for healing after the storms of life pass.

Whenever possible, I show people my physical scars. I have three on my arm from various falls, burns, and accidents, and one giant C-section scar across my lower abdomen that I brag "took three professional surgeons three tries to get this disgusting." In 2020, I received a rather large scar down the front of my leg when they cut open my leg, sawed off my bone, and screwed in my new hip. "This is where I received my bionic leg," I tease. "So, don't make fun of me. I plan to run the Boston Marathon one day."

I'm kind of proud of Ivar. That's what I named my new Hip. Ivar. Going through airports is a lot more fun. If you want to get through TSA quicker, tell them you are packing a large metal object under your skirt. That'll rush you right through the fast lane and ensure that you will always enjoy a nice full-body pat-down every single time you fly. I've started wearing sexier clothes to the airport just to make the experience more fun for me *and* the TSA officers.

Scars on the heart are harder to share, but they are there. There is no sense trying to hide them. From my early childhood, I had collected wounds and scars during my life that I had never dealt with, accepted, or named. Recovery and healing come from having the courage to own and name each scar:

My son is dead = my heart aches for him and I feel lost.

I had an abortion = I feel guilt, heartache, and anger.

My brothers and sister died so young = I miss them and worry about my health.

My dad and mom are gone = I have so many things I wish I could tell them.

I missed out on having a loving mom when I was young = I felt invisible. I feel guilt that I did not miss her when she died.

My marriages were disasters = I feel blame and embarrassment.

My ex cheated on me = I feel hurt and ugly.

I was attacked by a stranger and almost killed = I feel scared around strangers.

Two of my bosses sexually harassed me = I feel used.

There! Named, owned, and filled with Gold. These are a few of my Gold Scars. What are yours?

Naming what hurt you allows you to identify the emotion connected to it. Then you can forgive and address the loss face to face. In grief recovery, you create a timeline of your loss or trauma as it relates to a certain individual. This important step allows you to address the pain related to that individual directly. I don't mean calling the person and chatting about it. Many of the losses or abuses or deaths that occurred on my timeline involved people who had died. Two of my abusers were in jail. It is never a good idea to voice your thoughts and opinions to your attacker as part of your recovery.

I've guided others through this road to recovery. I can show you how you can get started "facing" the wrongs and wrongdoers. You will find my websites, additional materials, and contact information on my main website www.SylviaMooreMyers.com.

Healing from a Broken Heart
(Sweeping Up the Pieces of a Broken Heart)

We call it *heartbreak* or a *broken heart*. But these are misnomers. Heartbreak is not a "heart" injury. Not really. It's a brain disruption and affects your entire body. We can recover from most accidents and physical injuries in life, but a heartbreak is tough. When you truly have a heartbreak, you make mistakes. Life mistakes. Rebound mistakes. Your heart, brain, and ego are damaged.

A cheating mate can cause you to become toxic and try to win back the lost love by writing letters, emailing, texting, stalking them on social media, or even driving past their home. Believe me, I have heard some stories, and I am guilty of a few of these choices myself.

You will forget things, lose keys, miss appointments, and even act like a different person. Yes, this happens all the time. *Did our heartbroken friend lose her mind?* No, she has a broken heart, and her brain is reacting to the grief the only way it knows how.

Here's the kicker: The part of the brain that experiences withdrawal from addictions like nicotine, codeine, or Jimmy Dean is the same spot where we experience withdrawal from "love" or recover from our "loss" of another person. Addiction shares the same space with heartbreak. This is why normal, healthy people find heartbreak so painful and hard to recover from.

If you smoke or ever have, you know you have a problem. You try not to smoke, but your brain says, "You can quit tomorrow. One cigarette won't make you addicted again." These are lies your brain tells you. Your brain is a jerk when it comes to the roommates named addiction and heartbreak.

Heartbreak sneaks into that same spot in the brain and says, "Call him again and leave another message on his voicemail. Write him another long-ass letter about how sorry you are. Let's eat tons of chocolate ice cream and look at ALL the photos of him. Let's take sexy selfies and send them to him. Maybe his new girlfriend will see them." (I was spared the temptation of this—there were no cell phones in 1981). Or "Let's spend hours listening to heartbreak songs" (or just country music). "This is your fault. If you apologize the right way, he will take you back. He still loves you; you just need to prove your love." **Ugh**, shut up, brain!

Writing has always been my go-to remedy for what ails me. Putting your thoughts and hurts down on paper has an amazing calming effect. This writing is not a letter that tells your lost love how much you love and miss her or how the world is blah, blah, blah without him.

And no need to be a poet—just a simple "Dear John, I was broken-hearted when I found out that you'd cheated on me. I forgive you." Or "Dear John, I felt betrayed when I discovered all the lies. I am not letting this bother me anymore." Or "Dear John, I didn't realize you were suffering from your father's death and probably grieving the loss of our baby as well. I'm sorry I didn't see past my own grief and help you."

For goodness sake, DO NOT mail this letter to Dear John. But this is a fantastic way for YOU to address, forgive, and heal. Not to make amends with the person who hurt you. That day may come. But writing your thoughts down and moving through the emotions is *your* way to heal, no one else's. It's **your** scars you are filling with Gold—no one else's. I recommend a chat with me or another grief-recovery specialist so we can show you how to set up the timeline and how to respond to each type of emotion.

I have written songs and poems since childhood. After the Big John breakup, I co-wrote the song "Sweeping Up the Pieces of a Broken Heart". You can find a link on my website www.Sylvia-MooreMyers.com. The song expresses the torn-up condition of a heart cheated of love, and how plans and dreams are crushed by the loss. Sad, but that is how I felt.

My brain was addicted to Big John and didn't want to let him go. I was several years into my third marriage to James before I realized I had never let Big John go properly. Fifteen years and two marriages later, he was still hanging on like an old cigarette butt saved in case of emergency.

I didn't pine for him by that point. But I had never resolved the traumatic events of the loss of a baby and a marriage while still a teenager.

One day, out of nowhere, we were on the phone talking to each other. He was in North Carolina; I was in Georgia. We chatted for a while—after all those years. He wanted to apologize for the mistakes he had made. For the loss of the baby. I apologized to him for my blunders as well. We chatted cordially about our children from our other marriages—the rebound relationships after our divorce. He told me he still had a picture of me after all that time. I admitted I had one of him.

But, after the call, it dawned on me. I did not love him anymore—at least not the way I had years ago. The love I thought I had for him had long faded. The feelings I thought I might have if I spoke to him again simply were not there. The emotions were old emotions hanging around waiting to be resolved. They were shadows on the walls of my heart. My broken heart and the wounds had lost their sting somewhere along the way, but my brain had never gotten the memo. These were the first wounds that eventually became Gold Scars for me.

After the call, and after going through my own grief recovery, I was able to name and face all the pain and hurt from that relationship and others. Although the happy memories of Big John were still happy, the sad memories didn't hurt anymore. See, there is life after heartbreak! Goodbye, emergency cigarette butt! Hello, Gold Scars.

How did I do that? Losing Prince Charming was one of the saddest events in my life before my son's death. I faced it (courage). I touched it (acceptance). I brought it out of my brain and slapped it on the table and examined it (action). I realized my emotions for John were caused by his rejection and the abuse I suffered, and I wanted them gone. Your brain is an evil liar that masquerades rejection as love and abuse as need. Sorry, brain. I'm done suffering. Although "Sweeping" is still a good song, it is not my mantra anymore. I am still writing that new song.

Are you ready to get started on the journey to recovery? Visit my site and schedule a time for us to chat and then meet: www.SylviaMooreMyers.com. I will show you how you can tap into the secret weapon that helped me recover so you can begin healing. I've designed a workbook to help you through both the Gold Scars and 7 to Heal process.

I had been running from trauma and emotions since childhood. I left home at 18. I left town running at 19, and I kept running from the pain and everything else for years. As I said before, I was searching for an eraser, but the whole time I needed a highlighter. I wanted to forget, but I needed a better, safer way to remember. With the courage to accept my Gold Scar, I named my wounds, my losses, grief, and traumas and forgave or said goodbye to Prince Charming, my mother, Miss Clipboard, and myself (to name a few). I filled all the wounds with beautiful Gold Scars and walked away carrying only the memories.

I check in on Big John and his lovely new wife occasionally, on social media. I am happy for him that he is with someone who loves him. She calls him her "trophy husband" and I think that is wonderful. I am happy for me that I am happy as well. The pain and heartache are resolved. I'll call Adam a trophy husband if he would let me. Adam is my best friend and a gift from God.

When I think about Big John, I remember the cat, the pool table, our groovy second story flat in town. I remember we liked Little Kings Cream Ale and LaRosa's pizza. We both loved Volkswagen Bugs, and our dream car was the Porsche 911. When I look for something I learned from our very short marriage, I laugh that I can dismantle, clean, and reassemble Holley dual carburetors and help place them in an old Volkswagen Bug. If you must know, a decked-out VW Bug with Holley dual carburetors can go 95 miles an hour up a steep Kentucky mountainside (until you shoot a rod through the engine).

Be Creative. Here are some things you can do to begin Healing from Heartbreak, divorce, or a cheating spouse. Because heartbreak is a brain issue, we must show our brain how to heal. It's okay to add a laugh and a smile to the process:

1. Collect your falling stars and stardust. Write down happy memories of your lost love or mate (cat, pool table, VW Bugs, Little Kings Cream Ale, and so on).

2. If you are really hurting from an abusive relationship, SAY GOODBYE to butthead. Burn all the pics. Delete everything from your phone. Remove their name and number from your contacts list and block him or her for a while. This is an addiction in the brain, so treat it like cigarettes or drugs you don't want to take and get it out of your path.

3. Make a list of things the cheater did and read it to yourself every time you think you might want him or her back. Cheater, liar, bad breath, mean to the cat, whatever it might be. Make yourself laugh.

4. Skeet shoot the wedding china. Make sure someone is filming. Send me a copy.

5. Melt down the wedding rings. Or sell them and buy something fun like a cruise ticket to the Bahamas. If you sold my first set of wedding rings, you could get a lovely movie ticket and a bag of popcorn. Our house was robbed, and the thieves took every video we owned, but they didn't take my old wedding rings. Even robbers thought they were not worth pawning. Ha!

6. Throw darts at his or her picture. I recommend using the very expensive wedding photos.

7. Send the happy couple a wedding gift. I'll leave that one there. Nothing weird or dangerous. But can you imagine the surprise when they get back from the honeymoon and start writing thank-you cards, only to discover that they must write you one for the lovely Swissmar Chocolate Fondue Set (Amazon, $16.14). Please be sure to reply, "You're welcome, anytime."

8. Forgive the cheater. Yes, that's what I said. You must forgive. For that matter: Forgive the murderer. Forgive the attacker. Forgive the bully. Forget the abuser. If you want to heal, you must first forgive. You are still a child of God. Forgive the past so you can move toward the future.

9. Stay single (at least for a while). Rebounding from one bad relationship to another is dangerous. Trust me. I've been there. Adam and I waited nine years before we married. I had been pushed into marriage because of grief or insecurity several times early in my life, so Adam and I took our time. As a result, we are both very happy in our marriage. God saves the best for last, in my case.

10. On the staying single subject: Don't believe the lies your brain tells you. Don't repeat the pattern. You do not need someone to replace the one you loved. I see this all the

time. People divorced in January, married in June. I'm a little grossed out by the kissy-huggy photos on social media and couples talking about love and marriage when they just met a week after their divorces. Or worse, weeks before the divorce. Ha! Stop it. This is most likely lust, not love. This is rebounding, not true commitment, and the new marriage rarely survives the test of time. Love takes time. Give it lots of time. When you do get married, call me. I've never been a bridesmaid—only a bride. And a flower girl once.

11. Take time to be alone. Just because you want to fill the space the spouse or lover once occupied, this does not mean you should. Be alone for a while. God speaks to a quiet spirit. Plus, spreading out in a king-size bed alone or with your favorite pet is rewarding. Be a little selfish. If you need company, hang out with family and friends.

12. Pray. Get on your knees and ask our Creator to forgive you, give you a heart of forgiveness, and help you heal. Don't forget to ask for wisdom. God offers that one for free and gives it to you generously and without judgment (James 1:5 NKJV).

Healing Takes Courage

Healing can be a lengthy process. But I said before and I will reiterate here, "There is no set time for healing." The sooner you decide to take action, face your wounds, and accept your scars, the faster you will heal. You must have a little courage and want to heal, or you will live forever seeking pity or alternatives to healing that take away your life and happiness: alcohol, drugs, bad relationships, victimhood, drama, and even social-media addiction.

I have a "victim card." No kidding. The State of Georgia gave it to me after the murder of my son and subsequent attack on my life eight months later. I have that card and my private Victim Number, just in case the murderer or attacker is up for parole, makes a jail change, or I simply want to know the status of their accommodations. I hate that victim card and number, and I resent that I must have one. I am not a victim. Not anymore.

Similarly, I refuse to be a victim of my grief. Grief can hang out as victimhood and become toxic. Be careful. We live in a time of social media. I will not begin to name the concerns. You already know the world can look inside your home and bedroom if you let it. I see a growing problem with social media. It can become an addiction. If you are grieving or have been through abuse of any kind, posting a loss or heartache on social media for the purpose of rendering "hearts," "prayers," and comments from others is dangerous, and can cause anxiety and depression.

The act of reading the comments or likes from your post releases a chemical in your brain called dopamine. Sadly, the drug wears off quickly, and you will be checking the dang post every minute for the next few days to get another fix from that drug. (This behavior is not the same as smiling or laughing, which releases the same chemical.)

There is a deep emotional tie to putting your dirty laundry or broken heart out for the world to see and opine upon. Rejection is ever possible, and the emotional roller coaster is harmful. Not to mention you may be permanently harming your brain by impeding memory and reducing concentration. I predict Death by Social Media will be a real thing in the years to come. And, as a matter of fact, while I was finishing writing this book, I heard about a young man who took his life because of bullying that took place on social media.

Social-media addiction is a real thing. And the last thing a grieving person needs is another illness. Quitting social media is like kicking any other addiction:

1. If you can, just walk away from your beloved social accounts.
2. If you can't just walk away, turn off the alerts, beeps, and notifications from all social media.
3. Do not start or end your day checking your accounts.
4. Don't spend every break or lunch hour on social media. (Don't lose your job by checking it at your desk or service center.)
5. Don't wreck your car checking your account.
6. Avoid posting sensitive and personal information. Social media is forever. Even if you change your mind and delete the post, someone out there has already got a screenshot of whatever you deleted.
7. Get help if you have trouble breaking free. Social media can be an addiction. Treat it like one.

HEALTHY

T ake care of yourself. Good Health is the key to healing and recovery. Watching my weight, carbs, and calories, and even following the keto diet are my healthy tools. Exercise and limiting alcohol and unnecessary prescription medications are my secret weapons. Education, volunteering, and writing to help others are my gifts back. Thanking God and my family for standing with me through the healing process is a blessing.

Run the Good Race

I've been in two auto accidents in my life.

In 1985, black ice from melting snow covered the curve of a busy road. I was driving, and baby Jacob was the only passenger in my old station wagon when we slid off the road and onto the embankment. I pulled the large boat of a car back onto the road, and we came to a stop. Neither of us were harmed, but it scared me. Jacob slept through the whole thing. That's when I discovered the ugly station wagon I had hated so much was an indestructible tank. Wagon and I were buddies after that day.

The second accident occurred in the early '90s with little Isaac as my copilot. He was a toddler and strapped safely in a car seat. We were on our way to pick up Jacob from school. With my turn signal on, we were waiting for traffic to pass so we could turn in to the school lot. The teenager in the car behind me had no idea what to do when her brakes failed, so she just plowed into the rear of my stopped vehicle at about 45 miles an hour. The impact pushed my car forward a city block. Our bumpers became mangled together.

Isaac was unharmed from the event, but I suffered severe whiplash and permanent damage to my back, neck, and shoulders—injuries I would carry with me for life and pain I can still feel today. The day after the accident I woke to a fully dilated right eye. Having had medical training for our city volunteer life squad, I was certain I'd either had a stroke or had suffered some brain damage due to the accident.

It would turn out to be nerve damage, and there was no cure or treatment. Like David Bowie, I would always have one eye that looked different from the other, and I would always have difficulty seeing in the dark and in bright light. Back-and-forth with special contacts only masked the issue. I learned to forget about the eye, but I always must calm doctors down when they first see my eye at routine visits. "Not a stroke, just a broken nerve," I'll inform them.

"Oh, thank goodness," I will typically receive as a reply.

Sometimes, just to be ornery, I will allow a doctor to flash their little light back and forth, up and down, eye to eye a few times before I let them off the hook and explain. The time I make them suffer is in direct correlation to the time I spent in the lobby waiting past my scheduled appointment.

For several years, I would visit orthopedic and nerve specialists as well as eye specialists. There was nothing they could do but be fascinated and empathetic with my disorder, and medicate for the neck, back, and shoulder pain.

The last doctor I visited when we arrived in Middle Georgia ran a host of interesting and sometimes painful tests on me. He tested me from head to toe and made the determination that I might be showing early signs of MS. During the time I saw this doctor I wore a knee brace and wrist supports and attended many physical-therapy sessions. He scheduled more tests and medications for the following months.

My mind flashed back to Dr. Lavender, the cancer diagnosis and good ole Hazel with her "how to die" pamphlets. I knew what I had to do. I walked out of his office, placed the prescriptions, the wrist device, and the new appointment cards in the trash can outside his office and drove home. I never saw that doctor again.

That night, I called a good friend, Nicky Glover. Nicky and I had been writing music together with a group of local songwriters since my move to Georgia. He was an avid runner and one of the healthiest humans I had ever met. "Can I run with you and your friends?" I asked. The group of runners ran a 5K every Tuesday and Thursday and a 10K on Saturday mornings.

"Are you sure?" Nicky wondered if I was serious.

Although I'd run on the high school track team for a short time, I'd never taken it seriously. These guys took it seriously. I was facing a host of health challenges, including high blood pressure, anxiety, depression, and physical injuries from the accident, and I was barely 30 years old. "Heck ya, I'm serious." And I was.

So began the turning point in my health. Three months later, I was running a full 5K without issues. By five months, I was free of all medications, including blood-pressure medications. Thirty years later, I am still medication free, and I run a bit.

My point? The accident left me injured, scarred, and with permanent injuries I would carry for life. My choices were to follow the road of doctors, medication, and needles, or to take my health into my own hands. My decision to be as healthy as humanly possible changed my life. Don't misunderstand me. If running had not worked for me, medication or a combination of medication and exercise would have been okay. I let my doctor decide when it was time to reduce or remove heart and blood-pressure medication. Always chat with your doctor about your health. But I guarantee the doctor will have an easier job caring for you if you take your health seriously.

I'm shocked by the number of people who are convinced they are dying from some unknown ailment at the age of 30. I had started to feel this way in not dealing with my grief. I wasn't precisely a hypochondriac, but I was heading down that road a bit until I hit the brakes.

Whatever results the MS doctor had in mind were not results I was willing to accept. I didn't deny I was injured. I denied that these concerns were going to be a noose around my neck and take me out of this world too early or turn me into a victim. I wasn't running away from the truth. I was running toward the truth.

I thought I could improve my own health, so I did. If I had believed all the doctors and believed all the things I could NOT do, I would have lived within those boundaries—till death do us part.

Had I never started running or taking my health seriously, I would never have caved with my family, climbed up boulders, or swum through ice-cold underground rivers. I would not have given birth to my last son, Daniel or had the health and resilience to overcome the hardships of life that were on my horizon. It is a good thing I chose this path to recovery. I also found a new doctor who believes exercise and attitude are more important to recovery than medication.

Be Healthy

Getting in shape and staying in shape—even during grief and loss—are a matter of consistently doing things that you do not want to do. It is that simple. I offer advice on exercise and food all the time, and people make up the funniest reasons why they cannot eat healthy and exercise. Once you see the results, you will enjoy being healthy. Get started by doing the following:

1. Exercise. Exercise creates endorphins, serotonin, and dopamine in the brain and bloodstream—the happy chemicals naturally occurring in your body. Exercise sounds difficult, but a few sit-ups or pushups each morning is a good start. Add two extra every day until you get to your goal. Riding a stationary bike or walking on a treadmill is a great idea, but you can get creative. I have friends with trampolines, Bowflex trainers, and jump ropes. Do whatever you fancy as long as you are safely in motion.

2. Eat. If you have trouble eating, try several light meals a day whether you are hungry or not. If you overeat, then eat several light meals instead. Heartbreak and Trauma can cause eating issues. You might either eat everything in sight or eat nothing. Both options are bad. So teach yourself to eat properly.

3. Limit these carbs: white rice, white pasta, potato chips, white bread—they are all refined carbs. Corn is not a vegetable. You like it; I like it with butter or popped, but if you can make bread with it, it is not a healthy vegetable. I love potatoes, but they are in the same category as corn where I am concerned. Thus, a plate with bread, mashed potatoes,

corn, and a piece of meat is absolutely NOTHING to post proudly on social media. You just ate more carbs than a Big Mac with supersized fries and a regular Coke. Stop eating that way.

4. Study (not "Watch") what you eat. Google everything on your plate and add up the carbs. One Big Mac is over 48 carbs. Your daily carbs (unless you are an athlete) should be under 50 if you want to lose weight. I won't do a deep dive here on keto or any other diet, but I will say I am under 120 pounds and 60-plus years old. My weight and health are a direct result of studying my diet, counting carbs and calories, plus making myself exercise.

5. Stay active mentally. While it's great to stay physically active, using your brain every day is the best way to be happy as a result of being healthy. I am always reading or listening to multiple books. I constantly read the Bible and newspapers, and I keep current on all subjects that pertain to my businesses. My dad was mentally sharp up to the day of his death at age 86. He worked on a cross-word puzzle and wrote short stories every day. Just another jab at social media: social-media addiction damages the brain's ability to concentrate.

6. Consider your medications. I will not tell you to throw away your medication. Please chat with your doctor before making any changes. But I will tell you that you should know the exact reason you are taking a medication, the benefits of taking it, and most importantly the side effects. What are the alternatives to that drug, and is there a way you can avoid taking it by doing something else? I took blood-pressure medicine until five months after I started running 10K a week. My doctor immediately pulled me

off the medicine at my checkup. I was 30, and he said my vitals were those of a teenager. That was over 30 years ago, and my blood pressure and heart rate are still dandy.

HOPE

It's in Lamentations

The Book of Lamentations is so underappreciated. I used Lamentations to justify any "Mom Order" by warning my kids, "Hey, it's in the Bible!" If challenged with "Where?" I replied, "I'm pretty sure I read that in Lamentations."

But for someone grieving, Lamentations is the handbook. Look at this gem: "I will never forget this awful time, as I grieve over my loss. Yet I still dare to hope when I remember this: The faithful love of the LORD never ends! His mercies never cease. Great is his faithfulness; his mercies begin afresh each morning. I say to myself, 'The LORD is my inheritance; therefore, I will hope in him!'" (Lamentations 3:20–24 NLT).

The Bible recommends Hope over heartache: "Hope is knowing that God has a plan for us, not for disaster and pain, but for a future with Him" (Jeremiah 29:11).

Hope is that you will recover from your pain, loss, and grief. And after grief, three things always remain: (1) Faith, (2) Hope, and (3) Love (1 Corinthians 13:13, Sylvia version). The greatest is Love. Because you LOVE, you grieve whom you love. Because

God is Faithful, you have the promise (hope) of an eternity without pain, loss, or grief. God never lies. There is HOPE for you, your family, and your future.

It was right there in the ICU as my son died that I first saw a glimmer of hope. God's gift to me that morning. The story of the parents who'd lost their little girl to cancer. She wasn't really gone, she was elsewhere. And Jacob was elsewhere as well. I would see him again. I had Hope. It was greater than that. It was the darkest moment in my life, yet I could envision a brighter future.

You can have hope after a tragedy. You can have the hope that God will forgive you, heal you, and build you up. You can have hope for a happy future. Hope for a life everlasting. Hope for a healed heart, mind, and body. Hope that you can and should share with others.

Look. Hope is not the same as Wish. We all Hope that we will live a long and healthy life. We Hope we see our loved ones in the afterlife one day. But we *wish* we would win the lottery. To feel and have "HOPE," you must define that for which you are "hopeful."

I have a friend raised in an abusive home with an alcoholic father. Rather than following the same path, he became a successful, Godly, sober man with a positive outlook on his life and a love for his family. He said he hoped for a better life when he was a child. HOPED for a better life. Not "wished" for a better life. His eyes were on the target. He had a vision of his life in the future, and that vision became reality.

Henry Ford said, "If you think you can or you think you can't, you're right." Well, if you hope you will, you can. Hope is your vision of your life after grief and pain and abuse and loss. I am living proof that we can be positive in the face of grief, loss, and abuse. I could see the future because I never let go of the hope that my future would change. Oh yes, there were some dark moments, but hope always lingered about.

Right now, think about something for which you are hopeful. "I hope I can run again" was one of mine. And I did run again. Hope is your magic looking glass, the crystal ball to your future. If you can hope, you can do. No wishing. Just hope and do. Yoda *might* have said to Luke, "Hope and do, or do not without Hope."

Hope, Not Horror

Every human being on this planet figures out somewhere in grade school that life is going to end. You are going to die someday, and there is absolutely no cure for your inevitable "whatever it is that kills ya" unless you are raptured, or science discovers the fountain of youth while you are young enough and rich enough to partake.

You would think that everyone would be running around crying and screaming about their impending death. But, alas, we work and play and love (and cheat and steal and lie) all the way to the bitter end, in most cases not expecting death until it happens. The brain naturally protects you from fearing death to the point of despair. Although we all fear death to some extent, it's a low-level fear as a rule. Hope, in my opinion, is the counterbalance to fear, despair, and horror. And Hope is the secret weapon in recovering from grief.

Hope comes from Faith. God reminds you daily that He is there for you. You have Hope in the Lord. Hope for life after death. On the opposite side of hope is despair. Satan reminds you daily that you have no hope. If given a choice of Hope or Despair, I Hope you choose Hope.

When I was given the diagnosis of possible death from eventual cervical cancer, I turned to hope. I could have spent my entire pregnancy worrying about death, talking about death, complaining about death, and living the victim's life. (Thank God there was no Facebook in 1987.) Instead, I hoped God had a different plan for me. I hoped I could spend time with my new baby. I joyfully spent that spring, summer, and early fall with Hopes, not Horrors or Fears.

My Hope and faith, along with God's grace and love, conquered death.

Give Hope a try. What can you Hope for?

1. Hope to recover.
2. Hope your family can heal.
3. Hope God gives you peace.
4. Hope life will be joyful.
5. Hope for a better future.
6. Hope for forgiveness.
7. Hope to learn to love.
8. Hope to see your lost son, mother, brother, or lover again.
9. Hope for life everlasting.

The lack of hope is a sign of depression. Without something to hope for, it is difficult to move forward in your grief. Don't let the pain of your loss take away your hope. Of course, you can be happy again. Of course, you can love again. Hope is prewired in our brains, and without hope, we cannot live. Without hope, we would fear death until death won. If you fear death and struggle to find hope, you most likely have unresolved grief.

If you let your grief define you, then grief is what you will be known for, and this is NOT good. Let HOPE define you instead.

Let me impress upon you that grief recovery entails hope, and my specialty is dealing with grief. You can find resources on my website www.SylviaMooreMyers.com.

HOLINESS

Holiness Instead of Hopeless or Useless

After a tragic loss, we want to blame God. "Where were You, God?" or "How could You?" I drove 70 miles an hour with my convertible top down in 30-degree weather yelling those questions at God. I have never felt further from God and His holiness than just after my son was murdered.

It didn't help that everyone tried to convince me that "Jacob's work on Earth was done," "It was God's Will," or "God needed Jacob in Heaven." But blaming God and others will not help us recover. Separating from God will make you feel hopeless and useless and cause the journey to recovery to be more difficult.

When I lost Adrianna to abortion, I knelt in my parents' yard late one December evening and stared up at the stars. I begged God to forgive me and to strike me dead. He declined. I sang "Silent Night" and wept. There was no one to talk to about my pain. I felt rejected by God. My prayer life changed that day, and it took many, many years for me to get back on my knees to talk to God. I hope He missed me as much as I missed Him.

I'm just going to cut to the chase. We feel so far from God after grief and loss. We assume we are out of God's grace because we feel unworthy, undesirable, weak, and unprepared—unholy. We become angry at God and assume He crosses us off His list for bad behavior. We set unrealistic goals for God and ourselves, and because we can't reach them and He doesn't magically appear to erase the wrong, we resolve that *we* are the problem and God has left the building. We assume "loser" status as we have failed at grief.

We assume God sees us as weak, and now we are useless to Him as well. Hey, news flash: God loves losers. David (cheater), Peter (hothead), Sarah (laughed at God), Moses (murderer), Samson (playboy), Jacob (liar), Elijah (depressed), Solomon (bigamist), Rahab (prostitute), Thomas (doubter), Sylvia (baby killer). Still worried about your holiness in light of these losers? My guardian angel strolled to the front of the room when we both realized God was using my brokenness to fix others. "How's Sylvia?" "She's Groovy!"

Let God put the holy back in your life so you can recover and help others. God is not testing you. You found your way to grief because of the world, sin, and the circumstances in or out of your control. It was sin that separated us from God in the first place. God wants you to heal, but God wants you close to Him. And God wants you to pay it forward:

> Blessed be the God and Father of our Lord Jesus Christ, the Father of mercies and God of all comfort, who comforts us in all our tribulation, that we may be able to comfort those who are in any trouble, with the comfort with which we ourselves are comforted by God. (2 Corinthians 1:3–4 NKJV) Boom! There it is!

Being Holy or having "holiness" in your life can mean wanting and trying to be close to God (striving to be spiritually pure). We strive to be worthy to be in His presence. We teach, preach, and study in our circle of spiritual friends until tragedy strikes and we promptly demote ourselves.

I hate to throw anyone under the Church Bus here, but our churchy friends sometimes demote us as well. "Just let us know when you are feeling up to leading the women's group again, Susan." "Don't worry about the Missions Ministry committee, Bill. We know you have to take care of things at home." Uh, is Bill being demoted? Did Susan just get fired from the church-lady group? Do you think Bill and Susan will ever come back? Was that supposed to be a kindness? Nowhere in 2 Corinthians 1:3–4 do I see anyone asking Susan to step down from teaching because her husband just passed or Bill because his child committed suicide. Just saying …

No one is truly "Holy" but God. We are asked to "be Holy"—a goal. Paul explained that "But the fruit of the Spirit (God) is Love, Joy, Peace, Patience, Kindness, Goodness, Faithfulness, Gentleness, and Self-Control" (Galatians 5:22–23 NIV).

So whether you believe in God or not (and you should), to be a healthy spiritual being, you should practice:

1. Love
2. Joy
3. Peace
4. Patience
5. Kindness
6. Goodness
7. Faithfulness
8. Gentleness
9. Self-Control

Practice the goals FROM God to be close TO God. Meet Him where He is: in your heart. And you will be surrounded by His Love, Protection, and Holiness. Your wounds will fill with Gold.

HAPPY

LET YOURSELF BE HAPPY—it's okay, really. My family and I stumbled into many happy moments during our grief. They were as natural and normal as any other emotions we were feeling.

Jacob made it easy for us to laugh again. Standing around his bed in the ICU saying goodbye, we noticed the "For Deposit Only" bank stamps we'd all shared the day before. We laughed about those bank stamps for years. And we still do. The bank stamp on my brown sweater doesn't ALWAYS make me laugh—sometimes I cry. But I always remember how we were "a little happy" that day. His last day. Our last day with him … until we meet again.

Jacob was a comedian at heart. His rendition of Steve Erkle was priceless, and luckily, we have that on video. Memories of the funny jokes he would tell or the funny things he would do crack us up from time to time.

Thinking of the Corona T-shirt he wears under the stolen American Eagle shirt in his coffin always brings a smile when we remember how he promised not to buy a "beer shirt" at the beach T-shirt shop. I gave him the money to shop with that guarantee.

He came back proudly wearing his Corona shirt. "I said no beer shirts, Jacob." I was not happy with my teenager.

He proudly replied, "It's not beer, Mom, it's *Corona*."

Why that was so funny then and still funny today is beyond us, but the memory brings back the funny Jacob we knew and loved.

Bo was full of jokes and laughter every day that he lay there in that hospital bed. He was dying, and he didn't seem concerned. He knew where he was going, and he was joyful. He joked about his missing leg, called me by my childhood nickname (Tizzy), and told stories and jokes to the nurses and doctors in ICU. He had no possessions when he entered this world, and he had no possessions when he left. He was content. He was Happy. And this filled my soul with happiness.

Happiness Through Being Social

In this time of social media, you wouldn't think I would have to mention being social as a way to being happy. Social media is NOT being social. It's more akin to peeping inside your neighbors' home than being social. Social is having dinner at your neighbors' house. Social is watching a Little League game with friends. Golfing or boating or just sitting in the swing on my front porch chatting with my friend, Laura.

Have you ever met someone who you had been stalking for several years on social media? You know that friend of a friend who you officially know everything about? And finally, you meet! HA! It's awkward, isn't it? Because being online is not being social. Pen pals are not besties. They can become besties, but it takes face-to-face to take the relationship to the next level.

Be social:

1. Learn. Go back to college. Take classes online. Study abroad.

2. Donate your belongings, your time, and your talents.
3. Be a part of something. Join a bowling team, golf, paint by number, bird watch, cave, or do whatever you can to stay social and positive.
4. Get out of the house. Staying cooped up is not healthy. Thinking only about death and loss is harmful to you and everyone around you. Dress up, go out, and practice having fun again.
5. Try random outings. See a movie or visit family or friends. Shop at an ice-cream shop. Get your hair done or nails painted—just get out of the house.

The Fountain of Youth Is a Healthy Social Life

Recall I said that "Happy" is caused by chemicals in your brain, such as endorphins, serotonin, and dopamine.

Harvard did an 80-plus year study of 724 men, starting in 1939. The men were rich and poor, educated and uneducated. As the study continued, wives were included. Some men rose from poverty to financial freedom, and others squandered their wealth. But what surprised researchers the most were their findings on happiness.

As it turns out, people who were in happy social relationships in their 50s lived healthy lives well into their 80s and 90s. Likewise, the men and women who were isolated and lonely were less happy, and their health declined much earlier. Brain functions declined, and their lives were cut short in comparison to their happier, more social counterparts.

So regardless of your lot or loss, whether you're struggling with the death of a child or spouse, the loss of both your breasts due to cancer, heartache from the cheating husband you loved, or PTSD from trauma or abuse, let yourself be loved again.

Be careful; finding a small group with the same kind of loss or grief may cause the entire group to use this as a reason to live in the grief forever instead of taking the grief on the road to Happy. Grief recovery group is where you go to break "Free" of grief, not get "Stuck" in grief. If you hang out with single heartbroken women who swear off men forever, you may not be making yourself available to love again. If you want to fight, join the fight club. If you want to grieve all the time, join the grief club. But if you want to be happy again, well—find some happy people.

Go to church, go bowling, join golf clubs, attend social gatherings. It sounds crazy at first, but being social and having happy people around will make you happy.

Happy Helping Others

You want real joy? Real happiness? Pay it Forward. Help someone else. "Oh, how can I help anyone when I feel so bad?" That's the trick. That's the big secret to finding joy. You get more joy when you give out joy. You've heard the saying "It is better to give than receive." That doesn't necessarily mean money.

When I get a new employee, I have the last person I hired begin the training process. Why? Why not the gal or guy who has been there the longest? Because the process of having the new person train the newer person has a strange and wonderful benefit: When you are in teaching mode, you are in giving mode. You do not want to mess this up. Therefore, the teacher super-focuses on the job to be learned by the student, hurrying to truly understand the process before passing it on to the newbie. As a result, both employees learn the task more deeply and in a more focused way. The tasks the teacher didn't feel confident about before are now solidly learned. The new employee learns from someone invested in the learning. It's amazing.

The joyful heart GIVES to others. The process of helping other people will create happiness in your brain. Do you remember the last time you held a door open for someone? It felt good, didn't it? Yes, it did, and it should. The secret to Happiness and Joy is in the gift of giving. Get out of the house, drive to the store, and open some doors. (I'm pretty sure that's in Lamentations.)

Make Yourself Happy

These are happy things you can do that take little effort. You can go it alone, if you are not ready for company, or call a friend or neighbor to join you. But go do something happy outside of your home at least once a week.

- Visit the zoo, the aquarium, your grandparents, the park, or a neighbor.
- Walk your dog. No dog? Shame. Then walk your neighbor's dog. That's hitting two birds with one stone.
- See a movie with or without a friend.
- Have sex, with or without a friend. Ha! Made you laugh.
- Plant flowers. Or vegetables.
- Raise cute little chickens. (That's what I do).

It's the really easy, fun stuff that creates happiness. And that is what you are doing to help your brain. Super-easy fun stuff. On occasion, talk to someone who has a similar loss. Not the whining, crying friend who does all the talking and makes you do all the listening. I mean spend some time with someone you trust, chatting about everything including the death of your child, the loss of your childhood pet. Laugh about the stupid things people said at the funeral or the hospital or the grocery store. Comfort each other on occasion. Lift each other up. Then make fun of the things people said to you again.

- Every day, you should smile. Seriously, just smile. The brain creates those happy chemicals every time you smile.
- If you cannot find something to smile about, FAKE a smile. A smile releases neuropeptides through neurotransmitters (happy chemicals). I call them brain pushups.
  » Smile = dopamine
  » Smile = serotonin
  » Smile = endorphins
  » Smile = happy
  » Happy = healthy
  » Happy = not sad
  » Did you know that a fake smile can reduce stress, relieve pain, reduce your heart rate, and boost your immunity?

HILARIOUS

Can I Be Hilarious—Even During the Saddest of Times?

The morning of Jacob's funeral, you would think there was NOTHING that could make us laugh. Wrong. My brother and his wife, Sherry, booked a flight, and my brother's ex-wife, Kim, booked the same flight. They sat together, friendly as ever, with the common goal of getting from Northern Kentucky to Middle Georgia to be with the rest of the family.

When the flight attendant on Southwest Airlines learned this little secret, he had a little fun with the threesome. "Welcome to Southwest Airlines. Is anyone on the flight with their wife today?" James raised his hand along with many others. "Is anyone flying with their ex-wife by chance?" James alone raised his hand. Everyone giggled.

Then, James stood up and turned to the crowd of passengers. "My girlfriend couldn't catch this flight, so we booked her on the next flight down." The entire passenger manifest was roaring with laughter, and James retold that story in my kitchen with the exact same effect. We all laughed. Hilariously. And hilarious laughter is golden medicine.

Jacob was a riot when he was growing up. He made us laugh hysterically all the time. The memory of him involves so much laughter. It is impossible to truly "remember" Jacob without laughing your ass off. Boob pretzels, bank stamps, and office-chair drag races were a normal part of having him alive. These wonderful, hilarious memories are STILL a normal part of remembering him and celebrating his beautiful, wonderful, hilarious, short life.

Jacob snuck out with his buddy John one summer vacation and returned with a tattoo on his back. He'd wanted a tattoo even though we had said, "Absolutely NOT." So, in defiance, he had his initials tattooed on his back so he could conceal the new artwork.

When I discovered it, I started laughing. "Jacob, how are you ever going to enjoy this tattoo? You can't see your own back, and it will be backward in the mirror. Who is going to be behind you enjoying your tattoo?" We were rolling on the floor laughing about his tattoo then, and now we remember and laugh in memory of that moment.

Not to take death lightly, but isn't it easier to make fun of someone after they die? Mom, for example. My mother was so worried about keeping the family secrets. Now that she's gone … Well, she is fair game like the rest of my family. I find that incredibly funny.

I have five brothers and four sisters. I'm six down and five up. Smack in the middle. At least once a month, my parents left one of my brothers behind at church. Not intentionally, but they all looked the same to me and my parents.

One Sunday, my parents were leaving church with all of us children in tow when the pastor walked up to the window of our family station wagon (probably counting kids) and congratulated my parents on their recent anniversary. My mother explained that although she and Dad were married on April Fool's Day, "It wasn't the marriage that was a joke, it was the ten kids who came afterward."

The pastor laughed. "Well, it's good to see that the two of you are still so happy in love."

My dad replied, "Yeah, every time we are happy in love, we have another baby." The three adults laughed hysterically, and I never forgot that hilarious story.

My dad had always wanted to write about his time in Japan just after World War II. Dad loved the Japanese people and the families he met in Tokyo. His stories were fascinating. But besides entertaining us kids and teaching us Japanese, he could not tell the *whole* story because my mother was a very jealous wife. But when my mother died … my dad started writing, and he was not shy about his love life. Dad had fallen madly in love with a Japanese girl he'd met outside Tokyo while searching the hillsides for downed planes. When the young lady's father discovered the love affair, my father was forbidden from seeing her again by both her father and Dad's commanding officer. Dad was called home for a family emergency but planned to go back and find his love. That never happened, and his heart was broken.

Had my mother ever heard this story, she would have hit the ceiling, and somehow, we all joked, there would have been ripples all the way to Japan.

You are going to find and remember funny stories about your lost love, parent, or grandparent. Tell those stories over and over and laugh. Share them with the next generation and don't let the stories die.

Appa suffered from Alzheimer's disease before he died. His wife of 50-plus years, Amma, waited on him hand and foot, every day. Amma was a small, frail, and loving Christian woman. She had cut her hair short because she was so busy caring for Appa as well as her sister Judy. When Amma walked into his room with her new short hair, he said, "I don't know who you are, little boy, but I know you sure must love me." Amma loved to tell that funny story. I'll make sure Amma's and Appa's great-great-grandchildren hear this story.

John 2.0 and I were on our honeymoon, traveling across the country from Kentucky to Louisiana. At the hotel, a would-be romantic moment turned into hysterical laughter when 2.0 said, "You know, in this light, with your hair all messy, you look just like—Phyllis Diller." Oh, my goodness, that was so funny. I can never forget that gift of laughter. What a hilarious memory I will always have of that trip.

Find the hilarious stories, embellish them a little, and keep the smiles and laughter going. Tell jokes. Tell really bad mom jokes. My grown kids finish my mom jokes for me now—in public. And they laugh their butts off at me. You can borrow these until the Mom or Dad Joke Fairy gives you your own to share:

- When the waiter asks for drink orders, order the baby a rum and Coke—be sure to say, "Can he get a straw with that? He spills everything when he gets drunk." Look at the baby and say, "Better hand us those car keys, kiddo. You are not driving home tonight. Don't give me that ga-ga chatter—you are not the DD this evening." The baby will giggle, and the waiter will stand mouth agape.

- When the waiter brings the check, point to the four-year-old and say, "She's got the check—she's the only one at the table with an American Express Gold card." Then whisper, "She's a big tipper."

- The funniest moment came a few years back when I proudly announced to my family outside a busy restaurant that the beautiful purple flowers growing beside the door were "Phlox."

» The lady behind us rudely and loudly corrected me. "No, that is Lavender Lace Cuphea." I was taken aback. And I could see the "holy crap, that lady is going to die" look on Adam and my children's faces. But I held my tongue, and we walked around the corner before everyone started laughing. At me. Okay, I laughed too.

» Now, every time we walk past purple flowers of any variety, one of my kids will ask, "Mom, is that Phlox?"

» "No," the other will correct in their best mom voice, "that's Lavender Blah Blah Blah."

- **Help me, Mommy-Wan Kenobi, you're my only joke:** I'm a *Star Wars* fan. Yet I can't get past Leia's stupid hair buns in *A New Hope*. My family gets the brunt of my *Star Wars* jokes, because anytime I have two of anything in my hands (my favorites are toilet-paper rolls and challah bread, although I recently used two newborn kittens), I draw them close to each ear, grab the attention of the closest victim (family member), and recite, "Help me, Obi-Wan Kenobi, you're my only hope." My husband, kids, and now grandkids play this joke back on me all the time. I *hope* they tell this story when I'm gone.

HELP, HEALING, HEALTHY, HOPE, HOLINESS, HAPPINESS, AND HILARIOUS

Help, Healing, Healthy, Hope, Holiness, Happiness, and Hilarious are all connected. It goes without saying that the 7 to Heal Habits I suggested above are necessary for Helping you and your family, Having Hope, Feeling your worth and God's Holiness in your life, Being Healthy, Healing from loss, and being Happy and even Hilarious again. They are a package deal. If you really want to feel happy again, you must make Healthy and Happiness the Habits that give you Hope and Help Heal your broken brain, heart, and life:

- Be courageous, take action, accept that you are broken with all your loss, grief, and trauma and carry it with you. You don't "MOVE on" from loss—you "CARRY on." Go forth and let nothing stop you.
- Be unique, be yourself, be authentic inside your grief and loss.
- Forgive wrongdoing, forgive yourself, and forgive the stupid people who said all that stupid stuff at the funeral and afterward.

- Be Happy. Allow yourself to have fun. Treat yourself. It's okay to do something nice for yourself. Take time for YOU.
- Healthy means to thrive and flourish, grow with Vigor, Exercise, and SMILE.
- Be thankful. Be grateful. Turn denial into acceptance. Write everything down and Thank GOD. Anger, resentment, and pain separate us from God's holiness. Forgiveness, kindness, and helping others bring us back to His light. Remember, God uses broken people.
- Acceptance NOT denial—healing cannot hide. Bring it out and slap it around a bit. Look it in the eyes and address how it REALLY makes you feel. Go through a 7 to Heal process or the grief recovery program. No one can understand you more than someone who has lost as you have lost. No one can Help you more than someone who has been trained to do so.
- Shame is a way that you feel for something that happened TO you. Call it what it is, forgive it, own it, share it, fill it with Gold, and recover from it.
- SERVE others. To heal is to forgive others and to forgive YOURSELF, and to reach out and Help others learn to heal. Pay it forward.
- Get rid of doubt. Remember, Henry Ford said, "If you think you can do a thing or think you can't do a thing, you're right." He also said, "Obstacles are those frightful things you see when you take your eyes off your goal."
- Heal by being resilient Be an overcomer. Push aside obstacles and jump over roadblocks. LIFE is an obstacle. Real life has roadblocks. Lots of them.

- We are only ONE thought away from healing. One decision to walk out of a doctor's office and take our health seriously. One run after a fox to make him drop a chicken. One decision to put others above yourself. One prayer for forgiveness. One Smile to start to heal.
- Learn the path and methods (7 to Heal) for recovery. Hiding behind the victim is a survivor just waiting to happen.
- Fill those scars with GOLD. Own them, show them off. There is no shame in being human. We don't HEAL, we Scar Beautifully. Not Ugly Scars but Gold Scars. Be a Gold Scar Survivor.

WHAT HAPPENED WHEN I BEGAN 7 TO HEAL?

As I worked on my own grief, I began to dig into the many moments in my life from early childhood onward that had truly shaped the person I am today. Not all for the good unfortunately.

I had been bullied by a girl named Jackie in second grade. It was right after Grandma Clements had died, and I was trying to be Jackie's friend. Instead, Jackie hit me in the face. I ran and hid, and other kids made fun of me.

Years later, Jackie would outshine me on the ball field as I suffered her mean looks and snide remarks to the other players on our team. Jackie took the wind out of my sails for many years. I quit the ball team and never saw Jackie again.

With Jackie out of the way, bully number two, Tammy, showed up as the older sister of my best friend, Ann. Tammy was a hot-headed 15-year-old with a self-destructive personality. She was all about smoking pot in the back of the bus and worse. I made the grave mistake of turning her in to the principal when I was in the seventh grade. Somehow, she found out. When her detention ended, I found myself on the long bus ride home one day with Tammy sitting right behind me.

Tammy began hitting me in the back of the head, which at first, I ignored. Then, a few shoves later, she was in my seat, and my hands were entangled in her head of curly blond hair. We fought all the way to my house with the bus driver pretending not to notice. Why break up a good cat fight, right? Jerk.

By some strange coincidence, my mother was standing in the driveway, having just pulled the mail from the box, when I stepped off the bus with hands full of Tammy's hair, her blood or mine all over my clothes.

"Did you win?" Betty asked.

"I think so," I answered.

"Good," Mom replied.

Tammy and I never fought again. A few years later, Tammy died in a fire caused by a cigarette that set afire the couch upon which she was passed out. I had nightmares about her for years. But I always wondered how difficult her home life must have been to have made her so angry all the time.

There were other bullies in junior high. Twenhofel Junior High was notorious for morning fistfights. Teachers rarely stopped the carnage. So it was high school, tenth grade, before I got my mojo back. I informed my mother over the top of her *Cincinnati Enquirer* that I wanted to get involved in activities at school. She lowered the paper just enough to look in my eyes.

"What do you want to do?" she asked.

"Uh, I don't know, everything I guess," I stammered nervously.

"Then do it. What's stopping you?" she demanded.

"Well, a ride. Most things happen after school."

"You will have transportation." She ended the meeting, taking her eyes back to the headlines.

"Okay, thanks!" And just like that I joined every club and play and activity I could fit in my schedule.

My mother had never spent much time with me as a child. There were one or two shopping adventures I remember. Woolworths at Christmas and Johnny's Toy Store for birthdays, but usually nothing without my father and siblings. We enjoyed a yearly family trip to the drive-in, with lawn chairs and popcorn for the newest *Planet of the Apes*. I'm not sure how we all fit in that station wagon with lawn chairs. But the outings were memorable.

My oldest sisters were married and away from home when I was little. My sister Janet married and moved when I was in junior high school. Darla was my cousin. After her mother died, my parents adopted her. These were the women in my world. My dad's mom, Grandma Clements, died when I was young. Grandma Perky was never close to my family, although I learned years later that she was indeed close to my two dozen cousins. Whereas one grandma was nurturing and kind, the other (Perky) seemed to shove us in the other room every time we visited. I remember zero times sitting in her lap. I remember zero Christmas presents from her either.

My mother seemed to inherit this distaste for me (or so I thought), in that she was nurturing and kind with my baby brothers, but never with me. For the longest time, I would tell my young friends that I was adopted. Or that I had a disease I would probably die from before 20. These were, of course, coping devices that my child-self used to justify the lack of a mom. I told incredible stories to explain why my mom was not attending one event or another. Many were true.

I resented friends who talked about their moms shopping with them or accompanying them on trips or practice or whatever. I resented my brothers (all five of them) for having both my parents heavily involved in Cub Scouts and Boy Scouts during my entire childhood. I learned how to tie every rope and pitch a tent, and I memorized every Boy Scout motto. I did everything I could to be a Cub Scout and later Boy Scout, but I was a girl, and they were boys, and there was no way to compete with that.

Mom failed to show up for many of my school events. She saw zero of my baseball games. She attended zero sporting events. She went to a few of my marching-band events but volunteered in the concession rather than sit in the bleachers. I was field commander, received Miss Scott High School, became student council president, and joined the homecoming court on that field, and Mom never saw. I did notice that she wasn't there. Her absence troubled me as a child, but I didn't see it as neglect. Just lack of interest.

In addition to her obvious love of little babies and my brothers, she appeared equally obvious in her anger toward my sister Janet and later my adopted sister, Darla. My mom fought with them all the time. It was common for Mom to be in a yelling match with Janet or Darla. But Mom and I rarely spoke to each other. She didn't comb my hair or show me how to style it; she didn't paint my nails, pick out my dresses, talk to me about having a period, or even discuss boys.

I would have preferred to sit in her lap like my brothers did, but I would have gladly settled for an occasional fight like my sisters. I was a shadow on the wall. I once walked past two of them fighting on the staircase, and I'm not sure anyone noticed me. I was invisible. My brothers called me *the princess* because I never got in trouble and seemed to do whatever I wanted. But I wasn't a princess; I had a superpower. I was the Invisible Girl.

Despite this, I made all A's whenever possible, stayed on the honor roll, and got myself in the house before the streetlights went out each night. Dad had the streetlight rule, but neither parent gave me the "you must get good grades" speech. It was just something that was assumed, not verbalized.

I guess I was a mind reader too because I knew exactly what I could and could not do to thrive in a house with anywhere from six to ten people at any given moment. I would pride myself on being the only kid in the house who was never grounded.

My strength was in my dad. Busy as he was, and hard-working as well, he always had time to pick me up from practice (whatever it was I was practicing), take me on camping trips, and teach me to work with wood. He taught me everything from building to screening to planting. He gave me access to his vast collection of tools. Taught me to hit a baseball like a boy, fight like a boy, and defend myself from—well, boys. He escorted me to shop for dresses, shoes, and whatever else I needed for proms and other events. He was the mother I never had.

During my 7 to Heal journey into grief recovery from the murder of my son, I realized that I had never addressed the silence of my mom—until I had two conversations. The first conversation was with my eldest cousin. Mom had been buried for many years when my cousin visited me on her way through Georgia. She told me the story of a conversation Dad had with Mom about me when I was very young. Mom had been fighting with Janet since my cousin could remember, but not with my two eldest sisters, who were from my dad's first wife, so they were spared the drama.

However, according to my cousin, Mom was not happy about having another little girl. Janet was from Mom's first marriage, but my father raised her as his own. But I was officially Mom and Dad's only daughter together. My cousin didn't remember if Mom had done anything to me or not, but apparently at a big family event in front of my older siblings, aunts, uncles, cousins, and my grandmother, Dad told her to never lay a hand on me or else. And, knowing my mother, if she replied "fine," she meant "forever." And this may have meant no lap sitting, hair combing, or anything in between.

Whether or not this story is true is beyond me, but the next revelation came after Adam and I completed DNA tests a few years ago.

Spitting in a tube sounded easy. But actually, accumulating enough spit to fill the tube was onerous and disgusting. I finished because the joy of knowing if I was truly a Native American Cherokee princess, as told by my extended family, was only 12 weeks away once I got this bottle of spit mailed off.

I learned I was more a Scandinavian princess, and my ancestors apparently hung out with Moroccan, French, Welsh and English folks. I was more Cherokee than Elizabeth Warren, but a far cry less than I had been told. My great-great-grandmother was reportedly born on a reservation in Oklahoma. Her family walked the Trail of Tears and came back to the Virginia hills after she was born. Maybe I was adopted? Nope.

As my family tree started to build on the various ancestry websites, I noticed errors. My dad's side of the tree was lined up perfectly as expected. But all my cousins on my mother's side were classified as second cousins; my aunts and uncles appeared as cousins. There were mystery relatives I could not identify, and thus I made a phone call to my brother Jeff.

Now, Jeff was the youngest, so he had the most time one-on-one with our parents, and he overheard conversations and asked many questions. Here's the scoop that Jeff was able to discover through conversations with not only Mom and Dad but other family members. With the DNA test in hand, it appeared many if not all the rumors were true.

Mom was most likely the unwanted child of my aunt Ethel (the eldest daughter of Grandma Perky). Mom was born during a snowstorm in the coal-mining hills of West Virginia, and it was nearly two weeks before a proper birth certificate was created. Grandma may not have been thrilled about receiving a new baby to raise, seeing she already had a mess of kids of her own. And eventually, Mom was put in charge of watching the other kids as she got older, including one sister who was a year older.

At age 12, Grandma sent Mom to live with Aunt Ethel and her new husband. Life in the hills of West Virginia was tough enough. The family of 13 children was raised in a coal-mining town where shoes and beds were shared. Food was scarce during the Depression, and everyone worked if they could walk. Ethel and her husband owned a restaurant, so my mother learned to cook and run a business at a very young age.

My mother (Betty) was an exceptional student with a very high IQ and could have easily excelled in college. But rarely did poor kids from the West Virginia hills, suspected to be of Native American descent, get an invitation to college—regardless of their IQ. Upon finishing high school, she promptly married and moved away to Cincinnati, "to get the heck out of the hills," Jeff recalled Mom saying. She left the abusive man when my brother Bo and sister Janet were very little and met my father at the White Castle in Latonia, Kentucky. The rest is history.

Betty was rejected by both "mom one" and "mom two" as well as "dad one" and "dad two." To Betty's knowledge growing up, her mother was Grandma Perky, not her sister Ethel. So why did her mom send her away to live with her sister, who didn't really want her either? She was smart. She was a hard worker. Rejection by a parent can have a devastating result in the future and for future generations.

In my brother's words, Mom did the best she could with what she had. She never had a strong mother figure; therefore, she became a product of her upbringing. Her combative or distant relationships with her daughters were a result of what some professionals call "nurture failure." I call it multigenerational grief.

My half-sister and sister-cousin formed very close relationships with Mother when they were older, but my mother and I were more acquaintances in my opinion.

When I realized during my grief recovery that my mother had died with a ton of grief and loss and unresolved abuse, my heart broke for her. But I continued and resolved my hurtful relationship with my mother through my grief recovery and 7 to Heal.

Part of my recovery was in writing letters to those with whom I had experienced grief or loss. My letter to Mom, posthumous, was heartfelt with my gratitude for all she'd taught me, given me, and done for me, but also with forgiveness for the things she'd failed to do, for the silent years and the missed girl-talks. I asked for her forgiveness for not knowing about her loss and grief as a child, for thinking she didn't love me, for missing her funeral because I had a choice not to be there. The City of Taylor Mill honored the death of my mother with a full parade down a major highway, which she deserved. I cried.

It was intense, and the recovery from that relationship was life changing for me. I can't wait to run into Mom in Heaven and give her a big hug. That's the thing about Heaven—everyone gets fixed at the door. After my grief from my mother was resolved, I continued to complete my recoveries from the cheaters, lost loves, bullies, attackers, abusers, and even Jacob's murderer.

WHAT ABOUT MOM?

Three of my brothers are younger than me. I left home when they were in grade school and junior high. I mentioned to them recently that as a child, my assumption was that Mom ignored me and most likely did not love me as she did the boys. My brother Walt corrected me immediately. He said Mom bragged about me throughout his childhood and into well into his adulthood. To all the boys.

She subscribed to and saved every newspaper that carried my editorials and stories. She somehow remembered every one of my awards, crowns, and accomplishments when asked. I share this because I never understood how much my mother really loved me. She didn't "love" anyone very well. But it is comforting to know she did her very best. I complained to my dad once about Mother. He immediately replied, "You don't know your mother like I do. Under that hard shell of a woman is a giving and loving spirit. That's what I love about her." Wow, he was right. I didn't know her. But I do now.

Just before completing this book, it was suggested to me by a trusted advisor that my mother may have had ASD (autism spectrum disorder) aka Aspergers. I almost dismissed the idea until I was staring at a 200-question test. A test that would determine that I indeed had ASD and several additional tests later, a healthy IQ to go with it. It was like opening a door from a dark room. Every day of my life was re-lived with the idea that perhaps the reason my mother and I had very little interaction was ASD.

But it went deeper than that. I saw autism throughout my entire life – through every page of my book – every bully I met, every lost friend and relationship – everything. This revelation, no doubt, with be the subject of my second book. I won't go back and change a thing about this book as I know that grief, loss and trauma affect all human beings. And this book is about all of us. Not just me.

In summary, during my grief recovery, I learned all of this about my mother. Had I started grief recovery before my mother had died, I believe my relationship with her could have been very different. But I cherish the journey I took and the revelations I discovered on my path to heal. It was life changing, and a weight was taken off my heart. What a relief it was to finally fill those wounds with Gold.

CONCLUSION

This was my journey, where I learned how to have courage, carry my scars, and conquer loss, grief, and trauma. Through the 7 to Heal and Gold Scars methods I learned from real-life experiences, I learned how to love, be loved, and be lovable again. I was able to work through the abuse, loss, grief, and even my shortcomings to enjoy the peace of knowing who I am and how I can help others.

My scars are still there—just covered in Gold.

Part One: In my shared journey, I showed you how grief covers a broad range of emotions and prevents us from surviving, let alone thriving. From childhood bullies to domestic and verbal abuse. From lack of nurturing as a child to the great loss of a child. From self-loathing to physical attacks. From Stockholm syndrome to depression and PTSD. From blaming God to bargaining with God. If these experiences describe you, please know that I've been on this emotional roller coaster. I truly understand.

Part Two: I ventured down the almost accidental path that led to my recovery with the 7 to Heal, Gold Scars and grief recovery, and I discovered I wasn't weak, stupid, helpless, or a failure. I wasn't the Invisible Girl; I was Super Woman, and I just needed to find my cape and some courage.

Part Three and Part Four: I showed you how to begin recovery. 7 to Heal is the recipe for recovering from grief and loss, and this brought me back onto the path of living again. With Courage, a little Help to take Action to start the Healing process, being Healthy again, having Hope, feeling God's Holiness again, knowing true Happiness, and simply letting yourself be Hilarious, true Healing and recovery is a process that can be undertaken by anyone, regardless of heartache, pain, or loss. No matter how broken your bowl may be.

This journey should not be taken alone. So I offer to help guide you on your path. Visit me at my main website: www.SylviaMooreMyers.com, where you will also find links to 7 to Heal and Gold Scars.

Remember, I was a reverse Butterfly! The Invisible Girl. We start our life with such wonder and excitement. Depending on what life throws in our paths, we can get stuck in it, just survive it, or we can courageously take action . . . What have you learned? Can you see a different path? I hope you can. You can complete this transformation. And I want to help you be beautifully scarred.

On my website www.SylviaMooreMyers.com, I offer courses, free books, and guidance. You can order my companion study guide, schedule a chat with me, or sign up for Grief Recovery.

And Thank You for allowing me the honor to share my story with you. It was sharing my story that saved me. My silent years of not talking about my grief and pain out of fear of attack from my abusers and judgment from the world left me lonely and stuck. There is NO Grief greater than the one in which you are stuck right now. With courage, action, and acceptance of your grief, loss, and trauma, you have the hope of a better future. I'm here to tell you that you can heal with Gold Scars.

I'm here, covered in Gold and ready to Help. Contact me if you need to talk with someone right away.

At my website, www.SylviaMooreMyers.com, you can join other courageous survivors who are turning wounds into Gold Scars. We can share our Gold Scars with one another and help others find healing.

Sylvia

Do you need immediate help with depression?
The United States National Suicide Prevention Lifeline is 988.

To reach the Veterans Crisis Line, dial 988 and then press 1. You can text the Veterans Crisis Line at 838255.

Call the Teen and Youth Crisis Line at 1-877-968-8491. You can also text "teen2teen" to 839863.

ABOUT THE AUTHOR

I n her pursuit to heal from grief associated with the death of her teenage son, Sylvia Moore Myers discovered she still had many past losses, traumas, and a ton of grief she was carrying around. The wounds were deep and painful. The scars ugly and never-fading.

Sylvia began a 18-year journey to heal and learn all she could about Grief, Loss, and Trauma. She certified with The John Maxwell Team as a coach, trainer, and speaker. She worked through her grief with the Grief Recovery Institute (GRI).

But most importantly, she discovered from her own research the reasons we never really feel healed. She founded "7 to Heal" and "Gold Scars," which led her and others to discover the truth about grief, loss, and trauma. Now an Independent Certified Coach, Teacher, Trainer; a Speaker with Maxwell Leadership Certified Team, a Certified Advanced Grief Recovery Specialist, and a Certified Speaker with eSpeakers, Authority Speakers and the National Association of Speakers, Sylvia Moore Myers speaks across the nation sharing why healing takes courage, acceptance, and the willingness to be *beautifully mended*.

Sylvia and her husband, Adam, operate several businesses in Georgia, as well as a small family farm. Besides teaching, speaking, and coaching others through their own experiences with grief, loss, and trauma, she has published a children's book series, Ellowyn Noel O'Wyn, that teaches children learn to *Rhyme all the Time and Know What to Say When They Pray*, and Sylvia has 30-plus years of writing and editorial experience with weekly newspapers.

Sylvia is proud to now publish *Gold Scars: The Truth About Grief, Loss, and Trauma and How to Beautifully Mend"*.

A free ebook edition is available with the purchase of this book.

To claim your free ebook edition:

1. Visit MorganJamesBOGO.com
2. Sign your name CLEARLY in the space
3. Complete the form and submit a photo of the entire copyright page
4. You or your friend can download the ebook to your preferred device

Print & Digital Together Forever.

Snap a photo

Free ebook

Read anywhere

Printed in the USA
CPSIA information can be obtained
at www.ICGtesting.com
JSHW082107120424
61084JS00002B/56

9 781636 982823